Hillary is WETATi

Never Underestimate the Power of a WETATi Woman!

From the Perspective of an African Woman Leader

by

Ambassador Dr. Margaret Dureke

Author of 'How To Succeed Against All Odds'

JAHS Publishing Group

Publisher of **FACES OF POWER** & **Essence of WETATi** Magazine

"Read and Be Inspired"

Mailing Address:

P.O. Box 1164
Riverdale, Maryland 20738
Telephone: 301-864-2800

E-mail: info@jahspublishing.com
Website: www.jahspublishing.com

Printed and produced in the United States of America.

Library of Congress Control Number: 2016913255

ISBN 13: 978-1537494371
ISBN 10: 1537494376

FIRST EDITION

Written by: Dr. Margaret Dureke
Cover Design/Layout: Chidinma Dureke
Editor: Lynn Burns
Contributing Editor: Brenda B. Chavis
Typesetting: Lynn Burns
Publisher: JAHS Publishing Group
Technical Advisor: Wally Burns

About the Author

Ambassador Dr. Margaret Dureke is the Founder and President of the organization called WETATi and Margaretspeaks.com based in Maryland, USA. Ambassador Dureke has a B.A. in Political Science from Howard University and a Juris Doctorate Degree in Law from Washington College of Law, American University. She is a well sought after international motivational and empowerment speaker. Against all odds, she has accomplished so much with very little. She is a publisher and author of several personal and business development books. Her mission is to empower and DARE women and the next generation to DARE to achieve their impossible. She is happily married to her husband of over 30 years and the mother of three.

The purpose of this book is to share with, call to action and awaken African women and women elsewhere as to what Hillary Clinton's latest achievement signals. It is also to officially declare Hillary as a Woman who has Achieved The impossible (WETATi). From the perspective of an African woman Leader and the Founder and President of an organization called Women Empowered To Achieve The impossible (WETATi), I know a thing or two about what it takes to be a WETATian, and there is a need for an African perspective.

As an African woman leader, I wondered how Hillary's historical achievement might empower and inspire African women everywhere to DARE to achieve their impossible no matter where they might find themselves and with what cards life has dealt them. As an empowered African woman leader, as I've watched Hillary go down in the annals of history as a WETATian who has succeeded as the FIRST woman to be nominated as a presidential candidate of a major American political party, I thought that it is imperative that I share what this historical achievement may mean for African women and others around the world and to charge them to not sit back and complain or simply watch, but DARE them to achieve their impossible.

Every woman leader can learn from Hillary Clinton's strategic successful game plan for achieving the impossible in spite of the daily daunting challenges.

DEDICATION

This book is dedicated to a woman who epitomizes the meaning of WETATi and what it stands for and for her long suffering and unwavering commitment to ensuring that WETATi becomes a way of life around the world. She is a gentle soul who would give the shirt off her back to anyone that she can help. She is ONE sure constant reminder to me that WETATi is from God. She is a true Christian by the way she conducts and lives her life. She is dedicated, committed, focused, loving, nonjudgmental, supportive, endearing, compassionate, trustworthy and steadfast in all her ways. I call her my own "Mother Teresa". She is the Chief Operations

Officer for WETATi, Ms. Brenda B. Chavis; fondly referred to as "sister Brenda". My children call her Auntie Brenda.

Sister Brenda, you are WETATi and I salute you and ask that the world help me to thank you for your love, commitment and compassion. For the unwavering love you have for me, WETATi and my family which is now yours, I dedicate this book to you from the bottom of my heart and the soles of my feet. Thank you for loving me unconditionally. I truly appreciate you in every sense of the word. I will NEVER forget! THANK YOU AND GOD BLESS YOU.

THE WETATi SYMBOL

The above WETATi hand symbol is the unifying sign WETATi members use to identify one another, and thus is used throughout this book to hold each of the WETATi points of empowerment being discussed.

52 REASONS Why *Hillary is WETATi:*
From the Perspective of an African Woman Leader

Photo: Cleveland.com (modified by CHDesignz)

Never underestimate the Power of a WETATi Woman!

"I accept your nomination," as a WETATi.

WHO AND WHAT IS A WETATi WOMAN?

A WETATi woman is a woman that is empowered to achieve the impossible. She is a woman who can defy all odds against her. She is a woman who is not afraid to go where others would say, "not for me". She is a woman who is not afraid to be amongst other WETATians and respect them while holding her own.

"What does WETATi mean or stand for?" you may ask. Women Empowered To Achieve The impossible; and We're Empowered To Achieve The impossible is a global empowerment and educational network.

A WETATi WOMAN as espoused by President Obama bolsters WETATi's position and stance on who a WETATi woman is. WETATi is an organization I founded for the main purpose of DARING women, daughters and sons of Destiny and the next generation around the globe to push beyond their reaches in order to achieve that which is seemingly impossible no matter the obstacles and disadvantages ahead of them.

My story on how I became a WETATi and pivoted to dedicating my life to helping other women and the next generation become WETATi no matter in what far remote villages in the world they may find

themselves is written in one of my books called, *How To Succeed Against All Odds.*

For so many years I struggled to find myself in the marketplace after acquiring the degrees that society required of me and then realizing much later that I needed more than classroom education, to think outside the box, to create my own opportunities despite how daunting a challenge it is and to become an entrepreneur. After all, that is what I believe the American dream is all about; dare to go and do what others would say, "not for me".

I realized that most of the problems often stem from the fact that Africans are not given opportunities to showcase what they can do; I know that I have a lot to offer, though the opportunities out there are not for us. I had to encourage myself and came to the realization that I am empowered to achieve the impossible and that I can use this platform to help others who may think they don't have what it takes; therefore they settle for less.

I have been out in the field empowering women, the next generation of young men and women and the sons and daughters of Destiny for so many years. Right off the bat I knew that this line of work is what I was born to do. Hence, I decided to dim my light so that others could shine, and in disguise my light shined brighter.

Fast forward to what made me want to write this book about Hillary Clinton being a WETATian and the 52 reasons why she is WETATi. As one of my degrees was in political science as was my husband's, you can rest assured that we are both political animals and we follow American politics to its infinite number. We read up and are often glued to the TV as we flip from CNN to MSNBC. I am the CNN one; my husband is the MSNBC one, and to reach a compromise like people have to do in life, we will go back and forth between the channels depending on the topic and who the host is. American politics is fascinating to watch.

One fateful day, while we were watching the political events unfold on television, and things began to turn in Hillary Clinton's favor, and her prospects of actually achieving this positon was becoming more and more realistic daily despite the number of those who 'hate' her as they often say, a light bulb went off in my head and something inside of me said, "Hillary is WETATi." And I said to myself, "what is that, and what does that

mean, and why is that coming to me now?"
Then all of a sudden it came to me that
**Hillary is a woman who has achieved the
impossible (WETATi)**. Then I said, "oh wow!
Then what?" Then I heard a voice in my head
say, "write a book as an African woman
leader who has achieved the impossible in my
own right and share my perspective as to why
Hillary is WETATi and what that might mean
for African women and others around the
globe who may not be awakened to what just
happened for women around the world."

Then I got very excited and envisioned
the prospect of what Hillary Clinton's
unimaginable achievement would signal to
women everywhere and for African women
in particular because of the uphill battle that
lay ahead for African women who would dare
to achieve their own impossible in their
respective walks of life.

Though a couple of African women are
and have been presidents of a few African
countries, sometimes it goes unnoted or
unnoticed where it impacts on the next
generation or women elsewhere, but when it
happens to the country who is the leader of
the free world, the impact takes a different
shape and connotation and suggests endless

possibilities. It signals that it's a new day and new dawn, that women can do anything they want in spite of the difficulties they may encounter along the way because that is the only way women will continue to shatter the glass ceilings like Hillary Clinton.

I then juxtaposed the basic tenant of the WETATi woman against Hillary Clinton's characteristics and achievements and realized that she is WETATian, and hence this book and the *52 Reasons Why Hillary Is WETATi* from the perspective of an African woman leader whom other women, youth and children look up to, and I knew immediately that I needed to write this book and make my own contribution. I also want to say that though this happened in America, it can happen anywhere. As women continue to push beyond the glass ceilings, constructively support each other and embrace the characteristics of a WETATi woman, they are set to go for life and accomplish no matter what the 'impossible' may be at that time.

As an African woman leader, I think the hardest thing is finding other strong and confident women in their own right who will not hate but support and share opportunities where they are and become part of the *movement* and not become a *monument* which is often the case as if another woman's success will block theirs.

That is why I love Madeleine Albright, the former United States Secretary of State's statement when she said, *"There is a special place in hell for women who don't help other women."*

When I came upon this statement, it hit me like a ton of bricks. I didn't know at that point that women were that mean to each other, and for whatever reason I had no idea until later. It helped me to understand, and because of that quote I have a better perspective when I come upon women who don't make sense with the positions they take or don't take in any situation.

As time went on, I began to realize that I am becoming not just a woman who is empowered to achieve the impossible, but I also find myself as a feminist. As I researched the concept of feminism and women's empowerment further, I realized that they are very parallel and it's virtually impossible to be one and not be the other. In the process of this research, I heard on CNN that President Obama was interviewed by ***Glamour*** magazine where he described himself as a feminist. That information further heightened my need to fully affirm myself as both. If the President who is a man feels confident enough to identify himself as a feminist, who am I to shy away from it because of those who give it negative underpinnings.

A WETATi woman could also be a *feminist*, and for that reason I find this essay by President Obama with ***Glamour*** magazine to be poignant and a very good segue for this book on the 52 reasons Hillary is WETATi.

Glamour **Exclusive article**: President Barack Obama says, "This Is What a Feminist Looks Like."

President Obama and Michelle Obama with their daughters, Malia and Sasha, in 2015. *Photo: Carolyn Kaster/Associated Press*

"In his most extensive remarks about feminism, President Obama wrote an essay for **Glamour** magazine in which he reflected on American women's long fight for equality and called on men to fight sexism and create equal relationships.

In the 1,500-word essay, which was published online Thursday and will appear in the September print magazine, the President argued that 'when everybody is equal, we are all more free.' He praised the progress of American women over the past century while pledging to work on securing equal pay and reproductive rights. The President also warned against 'dated assumptions about gender roles.'

The President said that it was important to his daughters that he be a feminist, 'because now that's what they expect of all men.'

'We need to keep changing the attitude that raises our girls to be demure and our boys to be assertive, that criticizes our daughters for speaking out and our sons for shedding a tear,' he wrote. 'We need to keep changing the attitude that punishes women for their sexuality and rewards men for theirs.'

'We need to keep changing the attitude that permits the routine harassment of women, whether they're walking down the street or daring to go online. We need to keep changing the attitude that teaches men to feel threatened by the presence and success of women.' " – *President Obama* in **Glamour** *magazine,* written by DANIEL VICTOR, AUG. 4, 2016

This is relevant here because a WETATi woman is also a feminist and in order for both to be embraced, both must be synergized as one complements the other and lends credence to the other. By the same token, I would assume that the President would endorse, embrace and approve the concept of Women Empowered to Achieve The impossible (WETATi) because it further empowers women to demand what they deserve and have rights to and opens more doors for women in every sphere of life and business.

President Obama, for all intents and purposes, is a Goodwill Ambassador for women's empowerment and feminism like no other male has been in history. Women must take advantage of his endorsement of our power and come up higher.

The day the Obamas achieved their impossible.
Photo: Alarabiya.net

As long as I live, the image of this picture of Obama, his wife Michelle and their daughters will never die in my mind for many reasons. Apart from the historic reasons, as a mother of three daughters who were once the ages of Malia and Sasha, I can relate on many levels why their father, Obama, would take such a strong position on women's empowerment and feminism.

Hillary Clinton becoming the next President of the United States will heighten the President's position on the two concepts because she is an empowered woman whom I believe will do anything she can to advance women's empowerment and the feminism movement. Now let me state the 52 reasons why Hillary is WETATi and why no one should underestimate the power of an empowered woman as she can do anything she puts her mind to like Hillary Clinton.

52 REASONS Why Hillary is WETATi

1. She Dares to Achieve the Impossible!

A WETATi DARES to achieve the impossible regardless of her educational or non-educational background, socioeconomic status or geographical location and the other attributes which in most cases show up in the girl child at a very early age. When these traits are nurtured by a parent or guardian like in the case of Hillary Clinton or Simone Biles who just won 4 Olympic gold medals plus a bronze medal despite her unique circumstances, would give birth to a WETATian like Hillary and others around the world.

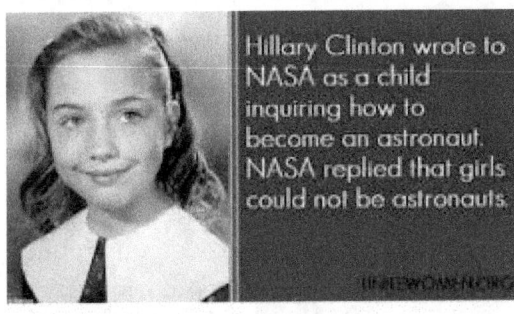

Hillary Clinton wrote to NASA as a child inquiring how to become an astronaut. NASA replied that girls could not be astronauts.

sidereaisandown

So she became Secretary of State instead

When Hillary Clinton wrote to NASA as a young girl and inquired as to how she could become an astronaut, they replied to her saying that, "girls could not be astronauts." How wrong they were, because "girls" have indeed gone on to become astronauts, and little did they know that the little girl who aspired to become an astronaut would one day become a presidential candidate of a major political party of America and is now on her way to becoming the FIRST FEMALE President of the United States of America. Hillary is WETATi. As a WETATian myself, I know that the only way to **achieve the impossible** is to believe that you **can** achieve that which many say can't be done and when you achieve it, 'they' now say, "WOW". If nobody has ever "wowed" you, you have NOT achieved the "impossible".

Hillary has "wowed" us many times, and therefore let no one ever underestimate the power of an empowered girl who later on becomes an empowered woman that in turn changes many narratives for women around the world. Hillary Clinton is WETATi because she DARED to dream the impossible and then achieve it. The world belongs to women who would DARE to achieve the impossible.

Instinctivemagazine.com

History was made by WETATi woman
who knows how to succeed against all odds.

"As a young girl, Hillary Diane Rodham's parents told her she could be *whatever* she wanted—as long as she was willing to work for it. Hillary took those words and ran with it. In a life on the front row of modern American history, she has always stood out—whether she was a teen campaigning for the 1964 Republican presidential candidate, winning recognition in *LIFE Magazine* for her pointed words as the first student commencement speaker at Wellesley College, or working on the Richard Nixon impeachment case as a newly minted lawyer.

For all of her accomplishments, scrutiny and scandal have followed this complex woman since she stepped into the public eye—from her role as First Lady of Arkansas to First Lady of the United States to becoming the first female U.S. Senator from New York to U.S. Secretary of State. Despite intense criticism, Hillary has remained committed to public service and dedicated to health care reform, children's issues, and women's rights. Now, she aspires to a bigger role: her nation's first woman president." – In *Hillary Rodham Clinton: A Woman Living History,* critically acclaimed author, Karen Blumenthal

2. She is Powerful, Enterprising & Embraces the Power to Dare to Dream & Achieve the Impossible!

To be an empowered woman, you must also be a dreamer. Without the power to dare to dream to achieve the impossible, you cannot achieve the possible, because the power to achieve the *possible* lies in the dream, belief and power to achieve the impossible. *The possible is buried in the impossible. Only a WETATian can excavate the 'possible' from the 'impossible'.*

This power belongs only to those who believe that *failure* is not in their vocabulary and believe that if they can think it, believe it, and act it, they can achieve it no matter the obstacles or length of time.

Hillary Clinton is WETATi because she is powerful, enterprising, dared to achieve the impossible and did it. Now many more women around the world will borrow on that dream of achieving the impossible in their respective lives. This will help move the women's empowerment and feminism cause further along around the world, particularly in Africa as a lot of work needs to be done and mindsets need to change in that part of the world to help women advance in every area of their lives. Sadly, some African men still think of and see women's empowerment as a fad, but as an empowered African woman leader, it's incumbent upon me and others to make sure that it is not so.

**3. She Sets
Audacious Goals.**

No empowered woman can achieve the impossible without first setting well-planned AUDACIOUS GOALS like Hillary Clinton has done throughout her life and career. She consciously tries to avoid drama as drama can dampen or even frustrate audacious goals. The Audacity to be yourself is Power and is Priceless! Audacity is the power to be yourself and live life by your own prescriptions despite obvious challenges and in the face of many adversities that often threaten these audacious goals.

To set audacious goals as a WETATian like Hillary, you must be fearless, confident and bold in the face of all odds against you and what you believe in and stay the course to achieve. If not, those "noises" or "distractions" will abort your goals.

Having the Audacity to be yourself regardless of what others may think of you like Hillary does, is POWER. The audacity to defy everyone and everything against you and achieve is powerful and priceless. Hillary Clinton has done just that and more as a WETATian. When your audacity becomes the thing that gives you the BONES to charge on and succeed against all odds, you know that you are a WETATian like Hillary Clinton.

Audacity is POWER when you USE IT versus just knowing about it. Audacity is not a RUDE attitude either. It is a self-assured Conscientiousness and Consciousness of who you are. It is a quiet confidence of whose you are; that you are not a mistake and that you are destined for GREATNESS IN SPITE OF...

President Barack Obama is proof POSITIVE of the POWER of the awareness of the POWER of AUDACITY and the priceless benefits of self-assured Conscientiousness and Consciousness of

AUDACITY to be yourself in spite of... Now Hillary Clinton is another proof of it.

To be aware of the POWER of AUDACITY is Empowerment knowledge, but the GUTS to use it for GROWTH or CHANGE and to DARE to achieve the impossible and affect others is PRICELESS. If you don't understand, ask President Barack Obama and now Hillary Clinton, the First Woman in the history of America to be a nominee of a major political party! My prediction is that Hillary will be the first woman President of America because the time is right and the time is NOW!

"When we stretch ourselves outside of our own confidence, when we are willing to live on the edge of our ability, there is energy, a drive that isn't present within the confines of a safe life. And using personal achievements as a catalyst to create opportunity for others is just as important. Fulfillment does not lie within the fountain of provision and safety; it lies in the joy of daring to believe in the impossible and risking everything to make it so—and then carrying others forward as a result of our own journey." – *Lisa Abeyta Founder/CEO,*

APPCityLife Inc. & Cofounder, Hautepreneurs and HauteHopes

Lisa Abeyta of APPCITYLIFE best sums it up in the above excerpt of her article. It is the GUTS to be and do without apologizing for who you are and how you came to be and what you bring to the table that makes you a WETATi. Hillary exudes these qualities as a WETATi and much more.

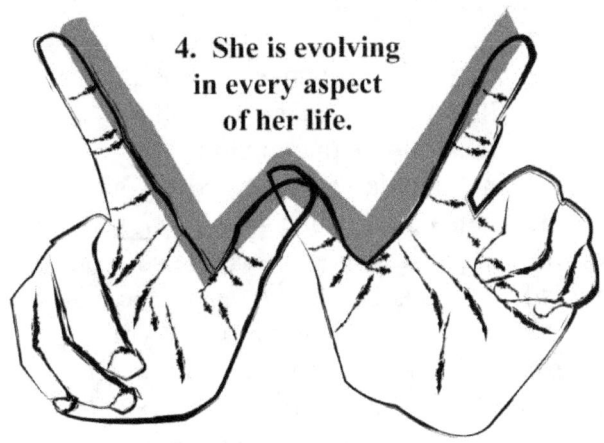

4. She is evolving in every aspect of her life.

The journey to power and self-contentment is a very slippery, rocky and slow trip. However, it is all worth it. At the end of the long, lonely, and at times frightening road, I found myself. Everyone should take his/her own journey in order to evolve, as Hillary has many times over, in order to find one's power. You may find yourself and life's purpose at the end of your journey as Hillary Clinton has. *She gave possibility thinking a chance and won.*

America is the only country in the world that I know of that will give you a chance to showcase your talent no matter what your last name may be or where you are from, despite the discrimination that we all know exists in this country. This is why some call it "God's Own Country". In Heaven, everyone is accepted like in America, except that in Heaven you are there due to God's grace, whereas in America you *must prove* yourself and often must overcome *many hurdles* to be accepted. Americans in general are so broad-minded in comparison to the rest of the world that the few who will hate or dislike you for no reason will have little chance to hinder your success. There are still a lot of people out there who will help you to achieve your goals if you push hard enough. Hillary Clinton has proven this frame of thought to be the case.

In order to evolve effectively, you must give up the *self-pity syndrome* and see yourself as a victor, successful, and not a *victim and a failure,* no matter what you have been through in the past, in order to evolve in all aspects of your life. I am sure we all go through things in life, some of it horrible and humanly unbearable, but as WETATians like Hillary we know that in order to evolve and meet our destiny or even flip it, we must be evolving in all aspects of our lives.

What you have gone through in terms of life's trials and tribulations may be different from what I have gone through. But the point is that even though our experiences are different, the responses that each of us *exhibit* to the situations most often are similar. Even in the face of scandals that would have aborted the goals of a woman who is not empowered, she has held steadfast, continuously holds her head up and looks ahead no matter what. Those things that happen to us that we often think are the worst are usually the things that define who we are or what we should be doing. The bad part of it is that they often come with a high price. Personally, I am grateful for the opportunities and my abilities through God's grace to turn my adversities into blessings and successes. That is what a WETATian must do in order to evolve all around.

Over time, however, I have come to appreciate adversities because they have helped me see the true colors of people whom I thought were my friends or those I thought were in my life for the right reasons. I was very naive at the time and could not have known otherwise. The good news is, today I am a full-fledged WETATian.

Whatever you do, you must stay the course, persist, persevere and press on to pursue your goals as you evolve. Be creative, intuitive, and proactive in your ways. Be determined to go the extra mile to achieve your goals and <u>stand up</u> for what you believe in. *Let nothing, absolutely <u>nothing</u> come between you and what you want.* Be determined to *succeed against all odds* like Hillary, and be ready to transcend above the adversities you may encounter in order to successfully evolve in all aspects of your life. Hillary Clinton has done this and is a bona fide WETATian. It is the GUTS to be and do without apologizing for who you are and how you came to be and the choices you have made that make you a WETATian. Hillary exudes these qualities and much more. She is a WETATian.

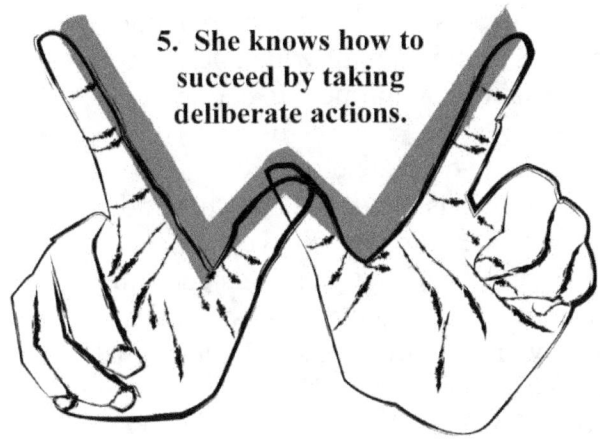

5. She knows how to succeed by taking deliberate actions.

Hillary knows about the urgency of NOW and how to take advantage of it as a WETATian. She knows that she is her own boss and CEO, and that she is responsible for her promotions or lack thereof.

No one can stop you, but you!

Success in any endeavor does not happen by mere happenstance. Success is a product of a series of deliberate decisions, conscious ceaseless efforts, determination, perseverance and persistence. It begins with well-thought-out and well-defined goals and objectives.

People with written goals are more prone to succeeding than those without them. The written goal is like the road map or compass to one's destination (a written goal empowers and inspires commitment to action).

When you write down your goals and dreams/visions, you must also think about how you are going to achieve them. When you write down your goals, it signals to your subconscious mind that it must get done. Hillary knows how to use deliberate goal setting actions to propel her successes and those of others.

6. She knows that if she doesn't have haters, she is not fighting hard enough.

As a WETATian, Hillary Clinton knows full well how formidable she is in fighting for others throughout her life and career as a

public servant, which has brought out a lot of
jealousies and haters along the way.

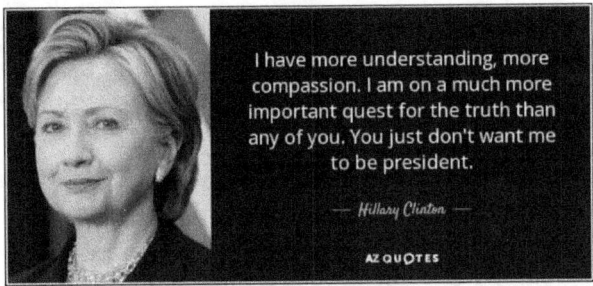

I have more understanding, more
compassion. I am on a much more
important quest for the truth than
any of you. You just don't want me
to be president.

— *Hillary Clinton* —

AZ QUOTES

Photo and quote: azquotes.com

A WETATian does not focus on the
haters but rather focuses on the reason for the
fight. A quick perusal of the life and work of
Hillary Clinton would shed more light on
why she does what she does and what
motivates her to deliberately act. Also, if you
watched the Democratic National Convention
and listened to the serious and heartfelt
testimonials of those she has fought for even
when no one is listening or looking, you will
see that she was born to fight for others. Does
that mean that she doesn't have flaws like the
rest of us? No, that is not the point of this
exercise, but rather to show that an
empowered woman does not focus on her
flaws but focuses on what she can do to

ameliorate hard conditions and use her power as a force for good for the others around her.

She is always serving to change the world in many capacities, and she embraces all cultures and is open minded about it too as a true WETATian.

Hillary deliberately takes time to read and empower the young and impressionable girls who are the future WETATians.

7. **She is loving, caring and forgiving.**

A WETATi woman forgives, cares and knows that love will always reign supreme. YOU MUST FREE, FORGIVE AND HEAL YOURSELF AND OTHERS TO SUCCEED.

Hillaryclinton.com photos

You cannot begin to love, free or heal your spirit and those of others until you have forgiven yourself for whatever you feel and perceive you did to yourself and others. You must also forgive other people or things that offended you that limit and cause you to feel unhappy or unfulfilled. Hillary is WETATi because she is able and capable of loving, caring and forgiving herself and others who are less fortunate and are in need of help whenever and wherever she can.

Photo: Alamy.com

Photo: hillaryclinton.com

Photo: hillaryclinton.com

Also remember that the etymology of the cause of one's anger most often lies within that person instead of without. If you do not take responsibility for what happened, you cannot begin to heal. It does not matter whose fault it was. Hence, without owning it, the spirit is still shackled and bound. The process to free one's spirit is a complex one and is different for everyone. If one part of the process is missing, the center cannot hold, and your goal to free yourself and your spirit cannot successfully take place. Also, note that there is no difference between self and spirit. That is why it is impossible to find self without freeing the spirit and vice versa.

To fully realize the true benefit of this process, you must not only forgive yourself, you must also **forgive others**. The reason is if you are harboring any kind of animosity in your mind, even if it is against someone else, you cannot completely free or heal your own spirit. Be advised though that there is a big difference between forgiving someone who offended you and going back to **'mess'** with them like before. Yes, you can forgive someone for what they did to you because it is the right thing to do and to help you free and heal your spirit. However, you should not forget what they did to you in the past. You do not have to be enemies with them either. All you should do is be civil and cordial with them. If you go back to that unhealthy relationship in the name of forgiveness, they will do it again. Deal with them and tolerate them as a Christian, but this time you set the **tone** and **scope** of the relationship.

For healing to take place, you **must first acknowledge** the problem or condition, forgive yourself and then begin the healing process. **(Allow God to work through you, in you and for you.)** God is not a God of limitation in every sense of the word and your level of spiritual consciousness of God during this process will make it faster and easier.

The process to free, forgive and heal your spirit is like giving yourself a *makeover from the inside out.* You see, when the inside feels good, the outside then reflects the inside. It is impossible to have a good outside without having a good inside. This is why you must start with self-examination first when anything is wrong before looking elsewhere for solutions.

It is entirely up to you to set the tone on how people should accept you or treat you. You should not ask for permission to exist.

Therefore, you forgive for your sake and for your **total well-being**.

To **<u>forgive</u>** and to **<u>forget</u>** are two different things, and one must not confuse the two or use them erroneously.

"However mean your life is, meet it and live it; do not call it hard names."
– Henry David Thoreau

No matter how I try to define courage, to really convey what and how I feel about courage, I do not think that I can do a better job of defining it than Henry David Thoreau. I truly believe that I live my life based on this principle. I try not to call my conditions or circumstances hard names despite what others might call them. Calling yourself hard names does nothing except depress you, reduce your self-worth, and get you to silently acquiesce to what others might be saying about you. First of all, you should not worry about what anyone is saying about you, because it may be biased and based on jealousy or some other human frailty. If you do not meet and live the life afforded you, you will experience misery and pursue being someone you truly do not need or want to be. So, in the words of Henry David Thoreau, however mean you find your life, meet it and do not call it names. Doing this really helps you heal and free your spirit to soar in all aspects of your life. Hillary Clinton exudes these qualities all around, and that qualifies her as a WETATian.

8. She is Not afraid to start over and is Not intimidated by anyone.

Hillary Clinton is WETATi because she is not afraid to start over and is not intimidated by anyone.

"They were all trying to intimidate us. They thought we would give up and not finish the work. But God made me strong."
– *Nehemiah 6:9*

To be intimidated is to be overshadowed and is an attempt by someone to diminish someone else's mindset so they feel less than in order for the intimidator to falsely feel bigger or better than.

One of the quick lessons I learned when I was into conventional network marketing is that a lot of the so-called leaders try to size you up and check you out to see if and how they can intimidate you and subdue you instead of adding you to the leadership group (this may not be your experience if you are not a leader). This was a sign of their own insecurity unbeknownst to them. Be very careful who you align with and who you trust. First, you must test them with small things, and in time and in some instances it does not take long to figure them out.

"Be courteous to all, be intimate with few, and let that few be tried before you give them your confidence." – *George Washington*

If you do not have a good spirit of discernment, you may become intimidated and get bitten before you know it. That bite does not have to be fatal unless you let it. All you need to do is learn very quickly from it, but do not retract from growing.

Once you allow someone else to intimidate you or make you fearful and/or make you feel less than and you let them get away with it, the GAME is over and you are finished. Whatever you do, never give anyone the POWER to exert that type of negative power over you. Hillary is WETATi because she embodies these attributes and more.

Be fearful of no one but respect all. The spirit of intimidation and fear can be reversed by adopting Faith and the Power of God in your life and empowering and changing your mindset.

"Success is not final; failure is not fatal; it is the courage to continue that matters."
– *Winston Churchill*

To dream is to be alive, and not to dream is to be dead. To dream and act is to succeed, and to dream and do nothing about it is to fail. The only time you fail is when you stop "doing" and continue "trying".

If you can't dream, you cannot envision, and if you cannot envision, you cannot believe in something bigger than yourself, and if you cannot believe in something bigger than yourself, you can never leave a mark in this world. No matter how many times you might have 'failed', you must not be afraid to start again. That is what WETATians are made of.

If you had a dream before, and somewhere along the line life happened and you gave up your dream, you owe it to yourself to dare to dream again, and most importantly you must believe in it, start over again and dare to achieve it.

There is no power in losing your power to start again, but there is a lot of power in going back to start dreaming again and hoping again because without dreaming and hoping that things are going to be all right, you will not have the impetus or the audacity and the right mindset to start over or to do anything after an adverse encounter that has dashed your original dreams and hope.

Believe in your dreams and dare to hope again, because it is the only true way you can thrive and overcome and go forth and become a WETATian like Hillary Clinton.

To lose your dream is not fatal, it is not failure, and it is the courage to start to dream again that matters.

When Hillary Clinton lost her presidential run to President Obama in 2008, she didn't throw in the towel; she reset the clock forward to the next opportunity without feeling despondent about the momentary defeat.

Photo: Upi.com

Hillary is patient, caring and forgiving and definitely not afraid to start over. After her ordeal with President Obama in 2008, she got over the acrimony between them, forgave whatever offenses she was feeling and went right to the field to support and campaign for the President.

A WETATi woman like Hillary doesn't have time to feel sorry for herself or to be bitter, because she knows better. She knew that what unites them is greater than what divides them, and hence their uniting for change for the good of the country is greater than both of them. Only WETATi women can do this without drama, and she definitely doesn't do drama, which is one of the main characteristics of a WETATi woman.

9. She is Not afraid to go where others would not DARE to go.

To be AFRAID is to SHRINK IN FAITH! To be afraid is to lose hope and shrink in size and stature of vision, and hope that something may go in disarray and turn out to be bad and give birth to unwanted consequences.

Most people never get to live a FREE life or the life they want and desire because of

FEAR, (**F**alse **E**vidence **A**ppearing **R**eal) when in fact FEAR is an important emotion if you know how to use it to your benefit.

To fear is to be ALIVE and to do it afraid is to trust yourself and the God who created you and has given you the power, dominion and authority to live a life fit for kings and queens which only belongs to those who DARE to get it despite the fear they feel, like Hillary Clinton. Power belongs to WETATians like Clinton who do it afraid and damn the feeling of fear that often robs potential greatness in people.

Once you embrace fear, it will dissipate and you become FREE to BE and DO. No one accomplishes anything worthwhile without overcoming the feeling of FEAR with faith and action. Go ahead and do it afraid and if you fail, get right back up and do it again because if you don't fail, you will not succeed and if you do succeed without failing, you will not be able to enjoy the success the way those do who failed before they succeeded.

"*Hillary* reminds us that women should not fear success or the trajectory into the public eye, because it is a powerful platform that can serve as a catalyst for the changes that women want to see in the world." – *Laura Arrillaga-Andreessen*

WETATi women are never afraid of being thrust into the public eye because they know who they are and why they are in the public eye in the first place, like Hillary Clinton. This is why I am smitten by her power to command the stage effortlessly and with quiet confidence despite the fear she might perceive. This is why Hillary Clinton is where she is today.

Photo: talkbusiness.net

10. She is DETERMINED and PERSISTENT!

Hillary Clinton is indomitable and impossible to subdue or defeat. She is a woman of indomitable spirit. She is cool as a cucumber but tough as Teflon. She is a WETATian. She is very determined and consistent, persistent and indefatigable in the face of a daunting journey.

"Nothing in this world can take the place of persistence. Talent will not; nothing is more common than unsuccessful people with talent. Genius will not; unrewarded genius is almost a proverb. Education will not; the world is full of educated derelicts. Persistence and determination alone are omnipotent. The slogan 'press on' has solved and always will solve the problems of the human race." *– Calvin Coolidge*

Photo: hillaryclinton.com

When you are a determined person, it means that you do not take the path of least resistance just because it is expedient which may in fact not yield the expected result. It means you stay the course to achieve. It means you become like 'Teflon'—PERIOD!

It is virtually impossible to become consistent and successful without being determined, persistent and resistant to the pressure to give up. In order to be determined and consistent, you must persist, persevere, resist and be inflexible to the temptation to give up or to be inconsistent in behavior or character from that of a determined or persistent person—if you want to be a person of integrity and success like Hillary Clinton.

"It was character that got us out of bed, commitment that moved us into action and discipline that enabled us to follow through."
– *Zig Ziglar*

Remember that "persistence and determination alone are omnipotent" and both will always serve you well if you DARE to stay the course. Hillary Clinton exudes all these attributes and therefore is a WETATian.

11. She knows how to SUCCEED even when people refuse to give her a chance!

If people refuse to give you a chance, how are you going to succeed? Hillary Clinton is WETATi because she definitely knows how to succeed even when people refuse to give her a chance. Some people cannot take rejection, but Hillary Clinton knows how to take rejection in good faith though not pleasant experiences. This is why it is imperative that people continue to reinvent themselves, **use all the impetus** in their being and constantly regroup, reinvent and readjust before taking the next step after disappoints or rejections or when a venture did not go as planned, as Hillary Clinton has done many times and now has mastered the art of it.

You must learn to be very resourceful if you must succeed. ***Though, if you defy the odds stacked against you and manage to find creative ways to get what you want, those who rejected you as a non-entity before will eventually come back to you.*** Hillary Clinton knows about this, and this is how she has successfully learned the rules of engagement in this regard and succeeded.

Remember, as they say, "in business, you do not have a permanent friend or enemy but a permanent interest." I guess this may be the reason for the phrase: "If you can't beat them, join them." I would say, if you can beat them, show them a new way. At that point, you then dictate the terms of the relationship if you choose to have one with them.

In addition, this may be how and why they say: **"you do not get mad, you get even in the marketplace"** and as they say, **"the sweetest revenge is success"**. Therefore, if you know that you have a talent, do not sit there and allow others to write you off regardless of the kind of edge they have over you for that moment in time. As a WETATian, Hillary Clinton has always known that this level of politics has traditionally always been reserved for men for generations, but she knows she can do it if given the opportunity. Hillary Clinton has changed this trajectory for women forever.

If we would reflect back on history and think about how the greatest people in the world achieved what they did, we too can rest assured that we can equally achieve the same or even more because the conditions and opportunities today are definitely better. I have also refused to buy into the notion that just because you do not have a certain advantage or certain predispositions such as, "your race", "your last name", and "your country of origin" and so forth, you then cannot defy the odds and succeed.

The things people see as unfathomable disadvantages and impossible bridges to cross, I saw as advantages and new avenues to set myself apart from others.

If you want to achieve the impossible, you must be determined like Hillary Clinton and her husband have been. That is one of the fascinating things about America; you must be determined. I personally think that those who feel despondent about their position in life and who think that those they see on television or other places that seemingly have succeeded in many areas of life just had it thrown upon them, really have not read up on how the families or individuals managed to succeed. Take Bill Gates for example, I am sure he was not born poor by most people's standards but he took a different path, paid his dues by believing in himself and defying all the odds, and succeeded in what seems from every indication to be his God-given talent. When his children grow up, they will not suffer as much as he did, and those who may not know the full history of Bill Gates' success story and how hard he worked and how determined he was, may envy the children. By the same token, Chelsea Clinton's life is better because her parents have gone before her and cleared the path. Her children's future may even be brighter because of their grandparents' fortitude. I also believe that the more obstacles you encounter and defeat in life, the better off you are in handling your day-to-day trials, which I know are inevitable for all humans of any age, gender, race or socioeconomic status. Hillary Clinton is no exception, and that is why she is WETATi.

Therefore, in order to succeed even when nobody gives you a chance; you must press on and stay the course. Be persistent to a significant degree if you are to find your true passion or calling in life. I honestly can say that I succeeded not only because I found my passion or God's gift for me; but because I stayed the course, was persistent, resilient and determined to succeed no matter what. I am confident that Hillary Clinton succeeded because she possesses these rare attributes of a WETATian.

I believe that if it is truly your passion and calling in life, like Hillary Clinton, all you need to do is to pour your heart and soul into it, and you will get the desired result over time; even if people do not support you. **"When you are dedicated to your work, when you're passionate in your beliefs— hearts will open and the world will listen." – author unknown.** So just "press on", don't look back, and never feel sorry for yourself, just like Hillary Clinton, and you will become a WETATi in the process.

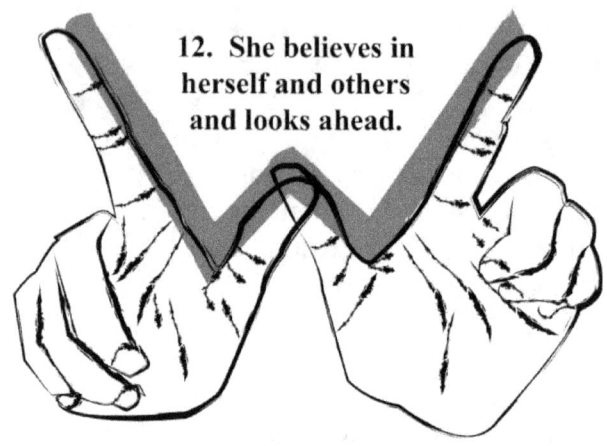

12. She believes in herself and others and looks ahead.

Hillary Clinton is WETATi because she believes in herself and others and looks ahead. The Power to Believe in Yourself and Make Things Happen is what separates a WETATian from the lot, and because Hillary Clinton has separated herself from the lot, she is now crowned a WETATian.

Whatever we desire to do or become, it all starts with our belief system and mindset. No one can achieve anything without first believing that it is possible. Success is like magic when you believe and work toward it.

The power to believe in yourself is crucial to making anything happen for you.

God has given us all the free will to do and to be, regardless of the odds we may face in our respective journeys in life. It is entirely up to us to choose our paths in life.

You have more power to accomplish your dreams and aspirations than you are allowing yourself to experience. If you are not where you want to be today, it may be in part because you are allowing others to determine whether or not you should be or not be.

The power to believe and achieve anything we want in life is within all of us. It is what you choose to do with yours that makes a difference. Remember that the book of Ecclesiastes tells us that Time and Chance happen to us all; it all now depends on what we each do with our portion.

So, what dream or aspiration have you been putting on hold for whatever reason or excuse? It is time to release yourself from mental sabotage, the manacles and shackles of excuses and procrastinations and bondage and begin again to believe and act, because it is possible and doable.

Personal Development NEVER happens Without Self-Empowerment! The magic begins when you believe you can do something.

When you believe that something is actually possible, you will be amazed as to how the ways to do and accomplish it will start to come to you. This is when the giant in you is both awakened and unleashed to go out and work for you. This is the opportunity God has been waiting for to show His might. The impossible becomes possible. At that point you don't need to fight for the opportunity.

"Yes, it may be necessary to fight for an opportunity, to struggle to break down a barrier to gain access to an opportunity. But stridence and friction will only get us so far. It is when we move beyond that struggle and change our mindset and become comfortable in our new role that we will have more confidence in ourselves and inspire it from others." – *Lisa Abeyta*

13. She knows her role
as a mother is the
most important job
in the world.

"My hero, my inspiration, my mother." – *Chelsea Clinton*
Photo: eonline.com

From an African woman perspective, the
most important job for a woman is
motherhood. Women are judged often on how

53

well they raise their children. Sometimes this could be unfair because at times the mother can do all that she can and the child may still not behave accordingly.

Hillary is WETATi because she knows that the most important job for a woman empowered to achieve the impossible is being a great mother. Despite the hectic and high demanding nature of her profession, she makes quality time for her daughter Chelsea. Over the years, I have intently watched from afar how poised, smart, respectful, thoughtful and very humble Chelsea is. Right from the time her father became President through today she has managed to remain out of trouble and does not act like a 'spoiled brat' as many would have done. She also appears to be compassionate and caring about others. Compassion at times **is** taught. I believe that she learned it from watching her mother throughout her life.

I am convinced that Chelsea became who she is today because of how she was raised by her mother. One of the ways you can recognize a WETATi mother is by the fruits—her children. This is not to say that if your child becomes problematic, you are a bad mother. Sometimes you can be the best mother in the world, and the child will choose a different path. However, the chances of the child going in the wrong direction are higher when you come from such a privileged background as Chelsea's and your mother is Hillary Clinton and your father is Bill Clinton. It is almost certain that her mother had a lot to do with the fact that Chelsea is very level-headed and doesn't seem to get ahead of herself in any situation.

Hillary Clinton could have stayed home to raise and watch Chelsea grow—after all she is their only child. However, like WETATi women around the world, she knew that all she needed to do is find *balance* between raising her daughter, being a wife to her husband and still having a great professional job; after all that is what our times call for. She has been judged by so many who may never walk in her shoes and even begin to know what it feels like to be Hillary Clinton. By the hard choices she has made throughout her life, she has vicariously empowered most of us onlookers.

In an article entitled, *"Why It Matters When Hillary Talks About Mothers, Daughters, Grandmothers,"* written by Emma Gray, Executive Women's Editor, *The*

Huffington Post July 27th, 2016 report during Hillary Clinton's acceptance speech, captured the essence of Hillary Clintons speech as it pertained to women, motherhood and daughters when Hillary said, "Tonight, we've reached a milestone in our nation's march toward a more perfect union: the first time that a major party has nominated a woman for President. Standing here as my mother's daughter, and my daughter's mother, I'm so happy this day has come. I'm happy for grandmothers and little girls and everyone in between. I'm happy for boys and men— because when any barrier falls in America, it clears the way for everyone. After all, when there are no ceilings, the sky's the limit."

Emma's obvious emotional reaction to Hillary's speech in this regard also showed that in some sense Hillary Clinton has become a universal mother figure to many, even to some who may never admit it.

A WETATi woman knows that being a great mom is the greatest job ever, and Hillary knows that the testament to that is embodied in the simple but powerful introduction Chelsea made of her mom during that convention in Philadelphia. In her Twitter feed in the same *Huffington Post* article, Chelsea reacted and said, "No matter the politics, I will not forget hearing, "I am my mother's daughter and my daughter's mother" sitting next to my mom, my inspiration." This apparent sincere and heartfelt comment about what and who her mom is to her bolsters and concludes this premise in the affirmative that Hillary Clinton is WETATi because she knows that being a great mother is more important than being a President of the United States. The good news is that she accomplished both very well, and for that reason I crown her as an official flag-bearing WETATian.

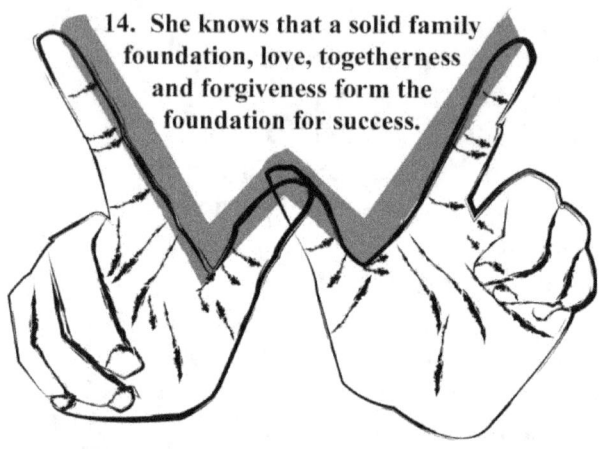

14. **She knows that a solid family foundation, love, togetherness and forgiveness form the foundation for success.**

Hillary and Bill Clinton at the Democratic National Convention:
"what God has put together no man can put asunder."
Photo: Deadline.com

There is power in forgiveness when it really hurts, and Hillary Clinton understands.

"In the spring of 1971, I met a girl...The first time I saw her we were, appropriately enough, in a class on political and civil rights. She exuded this sense of strength."

He explained how he was "too nervous to introduce himself properly at first, but that it was Hillary who approached him at a later date in the university's library."

According to Bill, Hillary told him that day, "Look, if you're going to keep staring at me, and I'm staring back, we at least oughta know each other's names."

"I was so impressed and surprised that would you believe it or not, momentarily I was speechless," he shared as the crowd cheered on. Bill went on to tell the story of how he proposed to Hillary "not once, but two more times before she would finally accept."

"The third time was the charm. I married my best friend. I was still in awe after more than four years of being around her of how strong and smart and loving and caring she was," the former President told the audience during his exciting speech at the recently concluded Democratic National Convention at which his friend and wife went on to make history as a prospective President of the United States 2017.

"Hillary is uniquely qualified to seize the opportunity. She is still the best darn change maker I have ever known."

Photo: eonline.com

A solid family foundation is the key to personal and business successes. I think that it is obvious by now that the love between Bill and Hillary Clinton can never be broken except by death because it has been tested several times and each time they transcend it and become stronger and form a stronger union than before.

Hillary knows that a solid family foundation—love, togetherness and forgiveness are the necessary elements for success for any WETATian. There is no way that she could accomplish all that she has without a very strong family support, understanding, and forgiving spirit.

From all indications though, Hillary may exude a simple façade, but she is no pushover. She just knows that in order to fulfill her God-given assignment on earth, she must always juxtapose the hard places in her life with the weight of her calling and then make informed decisions that would benefit their common purpose. It is often easier to sit and judge people when you're not walking in their shoes.

The power to forgive is the power to heal and strengthen the relationship.

The process to free, forgive and heal your spirit is like giving yourself a *makeover from the inside out.* You see, when the inside feels good, the outside then reflects the inside. It is impossible to have a good outside without having a good inside. This is why you must start with self-examination first when anything is wrong before looking elsewhere for solutions. Hillary Clinton knows full well that in order to become this formidable WETATi woman that she is today her family solidarity, forgiving those who have offended her, and forgiving herself for whatever she might have done wrong must happen. If not, none of these successes would have happened.

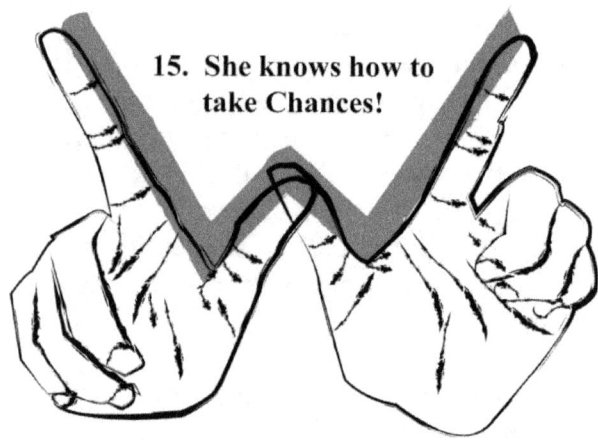

15. She knows how to take Chances!

Hillary is WETATi because she takes uncommon chances over and over again knowing full well that failing in some of the chances she took in the past is not fatal; they are only *necessary inconveniences* to the path of achieving her goals.

I believe that the worst chance to take is the one you didn't take. I would rather do and fail than wonder what could have happened. The sooner you fail, the sooner you succeed because failing at some point at something you wanted to succeed in is inevitable in life. It is unavoidable no matter which way you cut it. IF YOU HAVE NOT FAILED, YOU HAVE NOT LIVED!

So take some chances like Hillary Clinton so that you find your PATH sooner rather than later because you will fail at some point. The only question is when?

I know that to take a chance is BRAVERY, to avoid it is COWARDICE! *Success and failure are constantly at war and the one that WINS is the one that stays the course to achieve despite all the odds along the way!*

Everyone gets a chance. The question is what did you do with yours? Hillary Clinton knows when her chance is at hand and definitely knows what to do with it. Hillary is WETATi because she takes calculated chances.

16. She can do anything positive that she puts her mind to.

Hillary Clinton is WETATi because she can do anything that she puts her mind to. She understands the power of the mind and what can happen when one puts his or her mind to doing something positive with it.

The magic of being able to do anything positive that you want to do begins when you *believe* you can do it and put your mind to it. When you believe that something is actually possible, you will be amazed as to how the ways and means to do and accomplish it, even with no means in sight, will start to come to you.

This is when the giant in you is both awakened and unleashed to go out and work for you. I think that everyone will agree, whether or not you like Hillary, that her beliefs are *stiffened* in her belief system that she can do anything she believes and puts her mind to. When you believe, the impossible becomes possible. Hillary achieves the impossible against all odds because she believes that she can do anything she puts her mind to. Hillary is WETATi.

You have the POWER like Hillary Clinton to Rough-Hew your DESTINY in the direction of your choosing because God is no respecter of persons—despite the odds against you. Hillary Clinton demonstrates this quality too as a WETATi woman.

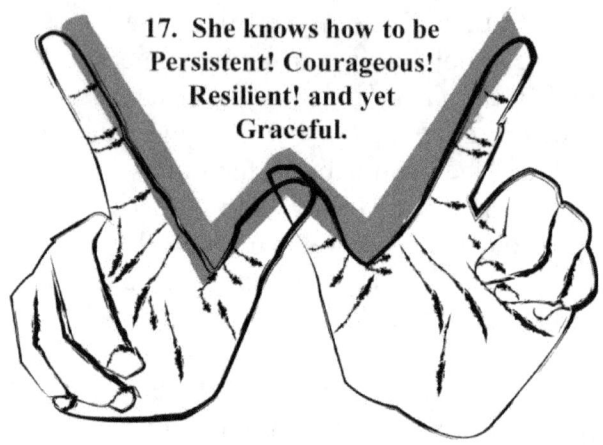

17. She knows how to be Persistent! Courageous! Resilient! and yet Graceful.

Hillary Clinton is WETATi because she is determined, persistent, courageous, resilient and yet graceful. **Persistence will break Resistance!**

What do you do when you get to the point in your journey where the rubber meets the road?

Do you persist or break? How you know what anyone is made of is by what they do when they get to the point where the rubber meets the road and how they handle it. That will determine if they DEFINED IT or IT DEFINED THEM!

TO PERSIST IS TO RESIST. To resist is to be empowered to advance no matter what. When you get to a breaking point or defining moment and you can't seem to go any further, you must resist the temptation to give up because persistence will surely break resistance if you stay the course. Hillary Clinton is WETATi because she is persistent, courageous, resilient and yet graceful. Hillary exudes all these attributes of who a WETATi woman is.

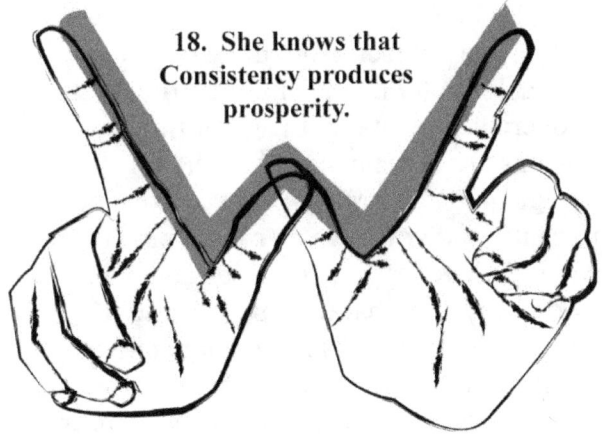

18. She knows that Consistency produces prosperity.

It is obvious to us all now that Hillary Clinton's consistency has produced prosperity in her life. When consistency persists and intensifies, prosperity in every sphere of your life manifests in abundance.

The reason for this is that the future of your prosperity is NOT in the hands of anybody, and know furthermore that promotion is from above and no matter what man may plan to thwart your destiny, it will NEVER happen unless you allow it (consciously or unconsciously). Be mindful, though, that prosperity is a "wholistic" state of being and financial wellness is only one single element of it. If you have your focus on just money alone, you will miss the mark because true prosperity is all encompassing.

So, free yourself from these manacles and shackles of a financial and spiritual impoverished mentality that your times or blessings are in the hands of others (or that your enemy is the reason why you have not 'made it') and you have no role to play in the matter. Whatever you do, never give your power away. You have the power; use it. Focus on doing what is right daily and when your time comes, the universe will conspire in your favor, and everything that was meant for your disfavor will be used for your good. That is the story of Hillary Clinton, and her hour has come against all the odds.

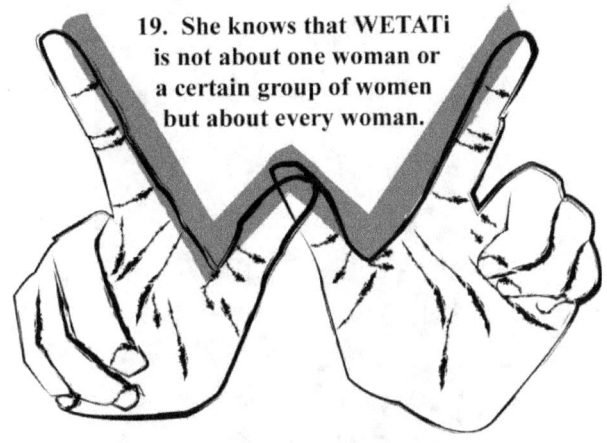

19. She knows that WETATi is not about one woman or a certain group of women but about every woman.

Hillary is every woman regardless of race, creed, culture or religion. As a WETATian she must see herself as every woman in order to be able to put herself in their shoes and empathize.

That is why Hillary is WETATi because she cared about all women when she borrowed the African proverb that states, **"It takes a village to raise a child"** in her book…

Photo from Amazon.com

From an African woman perspective, it does take a village to raise a child, and Hillary Clinton understood this concept way ahead of her time, and it's one of the reasons she is WETATi.

Hillary cares about all women and embraces all women. She knows that it's not about a certain group of women but must be about every woman as she is every woman by virtue of her position. Hillary is WETATi.

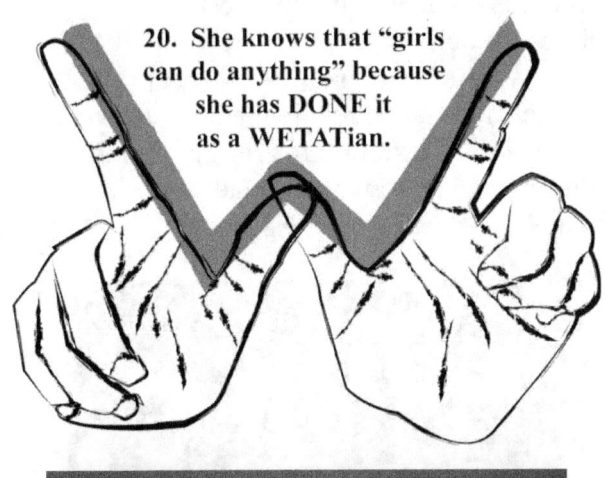

20. She knows that "girls can do anything" because she has DONE it as a WETATian.

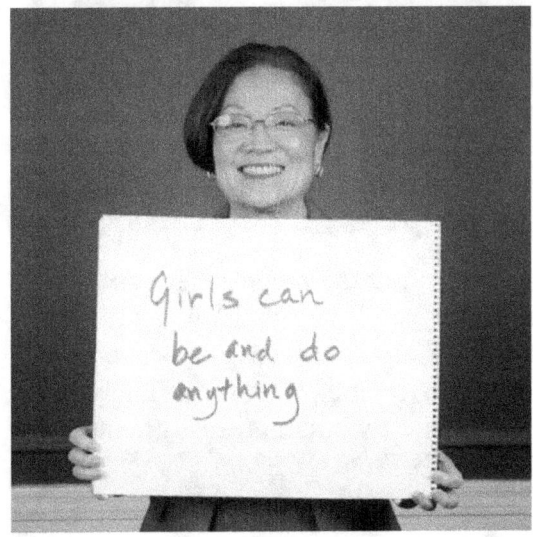

Photo: hillaryclinton.com

71

"A decade ago, then First Lady Hillary Rodham Clinton chronicled her quest—both deeply personal and, in the truest sense, public—to help make our society into the kind of village that enables children to become smart, able, resilient adults. *It Takes a Village* is "a textbook for caring...Filled with truths that are worth a read, and a reread." *(The Dallas Morning News)*

Hillary embracing and giving hope to a little girl like she once was that anything is possible and that the little girl can become a WETATian like herself because she has shattered the glass ceiling on the little girl's behalf in America and around the world. *CBSnews.com photos.*

"We just put the biggest crack in that glass ceiling yet," she proclaimed. "If there are any little girls out there who stayed up late to watch, let me just say that I may become the first woman president, but one of you is next." – *Hillary Clinton*

Photo: youtube.com

For more than thirty-five years, Senator Clinton has made children her passion and her cause. Her long experience—not only through her roles as mother, daughter, sister, and wife but also as advocate, legal expert, and public servant—has strengthened her conviction that how children develop and what they need to succeed are inextricably entwined with the society in which they live and how well it sustains and supports its families and individuals. In other words, "it takes a village to raise a child."

The way Hillary has raised her daughter Chelsea who has grown to be a very grounded and responsible young lady today and a mother of two children herself, is a true testament to the truism of this article.

"In her new Introduction, Senator Clinton reflects on how our village has changed over the last decade—from the impact of the Internet to new research in early child development and education. She discusses issues of increasing concern—security, the environment, the national debt—and looks at where we have made progress and where there is still work to be done." Hillary is WETATi because she is all this and much more.

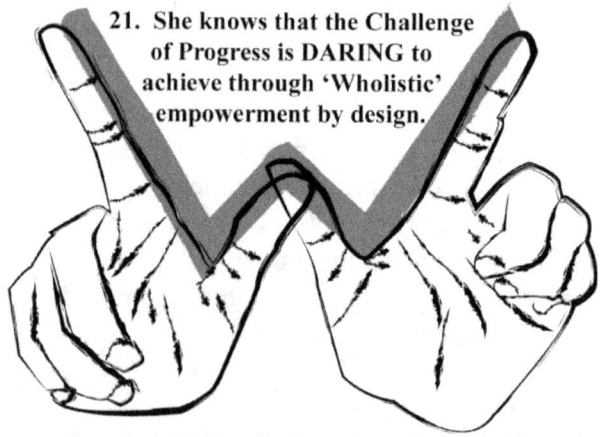

21. She knows that the Challenge of Progress is DARING to achieve through 'Wholistic' empowerment by design.

The challenge of progress can be good, long, hard, challenging, sacrificial and daunting for women pushing toward Women Empowered To Achieve The impossible (WETATi) ascriptions. The challenges have been difficult and at times seem insurmountable, unachievable and yet we must persevere because we are WETATians. We are Empowered to Achieve the impossible! The journey can also be rewarding despite the challenges that entangle with it. We are also developing personally and corporately as a result of those seemingly impossible obstacles that we encounter, embrace and face in order to overcome, like Hillary Clinton and many other women around the world have done in their own rights.

The face of challenge of progress is different for everyone and depends on who you are, where you were born, what you have or don't have, and how expansive your life and engagements in life, business and work are; and what one has allowed him or herself to engage in and experience will determine the level, magnitude of the challenges and the outcomes. Though life struggles are paved with so many challenges, uncertainties, disappointments, rejections, nepotism, racism and all the other 'isms' out there, a WETATian like Hillary Clinton still achieves despite the challenges along the road as she dares to achieve through 'wholistic' empowerment by design ('by design' here I mean road map; meaning that every WETATian must have a clear road map to be able to achieve the impossible).

Challenge is an essential Trajectory that makes progress possible because without the infusion of challenge into the fabric and embodiment of progress, it can never be truly measured and appreciated. The mere nature of the word CHALLENGE implies that there are some obstacles in the present moment or ahead, and that you must find creative ways to overcome if you want to experience progress. To PROGRESS is to advance from the present state to another state, in spite of the hardship at hand or that may be ahead.

For CHALLENGE to lead to PROGRESS and GROWTH, one must **DARE TO ACHIEVE progress and success THROUGH 'WHOLISTIC' EMPOWERMENT BY DESIGN**. When I think about what this means, Hillary Clinton the visionary comes to mind. Hillary is way ahead of her time and generation and totally embodies and underscores the challenge of progress and how she DARES to achieve the impossible through wholistic empowerment by design. Anything and everything about Hillary is progressive empowerment-driven and is by design.

Hillary understands the risks, discouragements, rejections, and disappointments, yet she *'Dares'* because she knows that if she faces challenges indefatigably, she stands the chance to own her freedom in every facet of her life. She also helps others to do the same. Hillary designs her life BOLDLY and 'wholistically' by the actions she takes and the ones she doesn't take. There are definitely many synergies between Hillary Clinton's philosophies and beliefs and WETATi.

There will never be progress without challenge. **There will never be progress without challenge. There will never be change without sacrifice.** There will never be progress without RISK. There will never be progress of a landmark proportion without facing challenges 'wholistically' and by design and without facing, at times, daunting obstacles. Anyone who cannot stay the course to overcome challenges will always play second fiddle to those who are able to do so and live a life of distinction like Hillary Clinton. Hillary is WETATi.

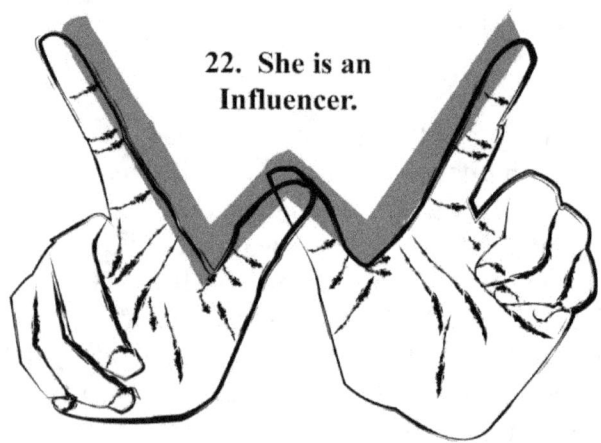

22. She is an Influencer.

A WETATi woman is an influencer, and Hillary Clinton is definitely one because her influence is not in question and she exudes that power in every facet of her life and work.

The first question here is who is an influencer and who influences the influencer like Hillary?

In an interview conducted with Hillary on her website Hillaryclinton.com, she was asked who influences her thinking and she said, "at the risk of appearing predictable, the Bible was and remains the biggest influence on my thinking. I was raised reading it, memorizing passages from it, and being guided by it." So from this statement one can deduce that God is her influencer. In addition, she also seeks the support of other women and men influencers to help her achieve her mission. A WETATi influencer like Hillary works with other influencers to bring about change or progress.

Photo: Bustele.com

Hillary Clinton's influence around the world, from her early years working as an advocate for children and women's rights, to being the First Lady of America and to becoming the first female President of America; there is no shortage of evidence of her influence in every aspect of her life and work.

Photo: Hollywood Reporter.com

As a WETATi woman her influence is not just here in America but around the globe, and she knows it, and I believe that is why she is very cautious in all her ways because she knows that everything she does or doesn't do will impact those she influences directly or indirectly, intentionally or unintentionally.

An influencer is one who has the ability to influence the behavior or opinions of others like Hillary. An influencer like Clinton becomes an advocate for a lot of good causes through the power of her gained influence over time.

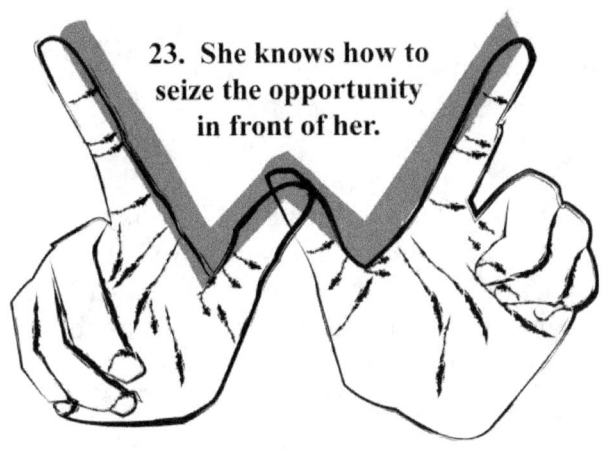

23. She knows how to seize the opportunity in front of her.

"Hillary is uniquely qualified to **seize** the opportunity. She is still the best darn change maker I have ever known." – *Bill Clinton*

When an opportunity presents itself, if it is NOT INCONVENIENT, it is not an Opportunity of Landmark Proportions. Hillary Clinton knows this too as her whole life has been surrounded with several loops of inconvenient opportunities that she would often seize despite the inconvenience that they might be fraught with. These series of inconvenient opportunities that Hillary Clinton has managed to flip for good are the hallmark of anyone who knows how to seize the opportunity (opportunity does not always have to be positive on its face) in front of them. This is why as a WETATian, Clinton has almost always turned them into opportunities of landmark proportions.

WETATians always defy the challenges in the midst of the opportunity. This means that it is one's ability to juxtapose the two and take action despite the inconvenience that will give one the BREAK one is looking for. If you are not looking for an opportunity, it will get you out of the place of excuses and propel you to the level where you make things HAPPEN and NOT make EXCUSES!

What you believe, you STAND for. The company you keep will determine how far you go in life and in seizing the opportunities in front of you like Hillary Clinton has done many times over.

Hillary Clinton, as a WETATian, does not make excuses; she seizes the moment each and every time the opportunity presents itself as she creates history, and by doing that she challenges other women everywhere to do the same in their respective fields and across the globe.

"Can Hillary Clinton Seize the Moment In Historic Acceptance Speech?";
on nbcnews.com/storyline/2016-conventions/can-hillary-clinton-seize-moment-historic-acceptance-speech. BY ALEX SEITZ-WALD;
was the question and the majority agreed that indeed she not only
seized the moment but will go down in the annals of history as such.

Hillary knew without a doubt that it was her lifetime's biggest opportunity and understood the magnitude of it and why she must seize the moment now or never, and because she is a WETATi, she knows it is her time.

When something is called an opportunity, it is because some may not see it as such because if everyone sees it as such, it will no longer be an opportunity. Hillary Clinton is able to decipher many hard places in life as opportunities way before others see them because she is a WETATian.

24. She knows that her greatest opponent when managed well could be her greatest ally.

What divided them has now **UNITED** them. They both now have become **WINNERS.** *Photo: Deadline.com*

She is both socially conscious and responsible. Hillary is WETATi because she is socially and actively conscious and responsible. She has a zeal for life, and her passion and determination to transform the lives of women and to see women liberated from the ills of life such as human trafficking, domestic abuse, low self-esteem, and lack of educational opportunities has been noted nationally and internationally throughout her life and career. She believes in economic opportunity for all with a special interest for women as a WETATian. There are very few people who actually put action to their dreams and soar. Hillary Clinton is one of those people. Since her career as a young lawyer, she has made tireless efforts to empower women and children in many facets of life including balancing family and work.

She has helped to breathe new life into many efforts to fine-tune the leadership of young women across the globe. She moves seamlessly across the boundaries of cultures and ethnic diversities. She has highlighted the work of women on an international level by knowing how to gracefully arise from her pain and profit from it.

Topnews.in

The history between President Obama and Hillary Clinton is no secret and Hillary has strategically managed it well and like the WETATian she is, turned every 'enemy' or opponent and some foes to be her greatest allies. That is what you do when you are an empowered woman like she is. Even though both Hillary Clinton and President Obama put on their boxing gloves in 2008 during their very contested and bitter campaign, they were able to put their differences aside and focus on the nation's needs and work for the common good of the people.

Most people thought it was over for the two of them, but a WETATian like Hillary Clinton knows that her greatest opponent when managed well can become her greatest ally. In her case, it happened. She did not only WIN with Obama, she also WON with Bernie Sanders despite what and how the political pundits said was going to be the end result. The end result of the political fights between Obama and Clinton and Clinton and Sanders is simply a thing of beauty and should be emulated by others in the political world. They all fought a good fight and made history but resolved their conflicts amicably behind closed doors in the interest of the party and country; not personally.

The power in fighting or conflict is not the act itself but rather how well we resolve it and unite for the common goal. Hillary also proves, like the WETATian that she is, that the essence of conflict is not to distance people but to bring people together for the good of all.

Hillary Clinton with her former opponent Bernie Sanders
UNITED as one and moving the people's agenda forward.
AP Photo/David Goldman

25. She knows that in life and business, you don't get what you deserve. You only get what you NEGOTIATE and MAKE HAPPEN.

A WETATi woman knows this fact, and the way Hillary Clinton worked with both President Obama and Bernie Sanders proves that she knows very well that her success will not only depend on thinking that she deserves it because she is qualified for the position, but on her power to negotiate and make things work with both men and will play a major role on how and what she gets and deserves.

Hillary is aware that inaction is a form of negotiation. At times she strategically stayed inactive as part of her negotiating power because she knows that in life and business there is a time to speak and a time to not speak. A WETATi woman knows and uses it to her advantage when needed. Hillary Clinton is the epitome of who a WETATi woman is. She knows that in life and business she doesn't get what she deserves, but what she negotiates and makes happen.

Passivity is a form of negotiation. Taking action when you are supposed to is a form of negotiation and a way of making things happen. Prayer is a form of making things happen and negotiating what you deserve in life or business. Sleeping too much is a form of negotiation. Gossiping is a form of negotiating your path in life. Minding other people's business instead of your own is a form of negotiation.

Going beyond the call of duty is a form of negotiation and making things happen, etc. Be aware also that if you did nothing, you still participated even if you didn't know it. For example, some people will say, "I don't care about voting because it does not matter." Wrong! Voting is a form of you exercising your right and negotiating in the political corridors that in turn translates into economic consequences—positively or negatively—in the society in which you reside and which determines your economic well-being.

Just because you refuse to constructively engage does not mean that you did not engage. If everyone was to get what they deserve without active participation, we would be living in a utopian society. Hillary is WETATi because she has done it successfully.

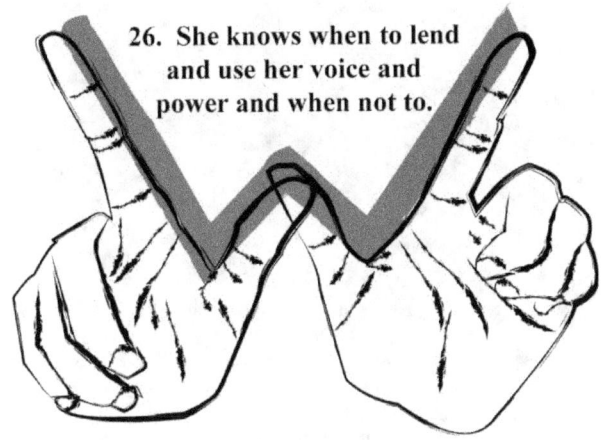

26. She knows when to lend and use her voice and power and when not to.

Like Hillary Clinton, WETATi women often intuitively know when they should lend their power and voices in order to make a difference in causes. In fact, her whole life is marked by such deeds privately and publically.

There are definitely no shortage of places to find what she has done to lend her voice, power and influence as a WETATi woman to help others. It is literarily what she has done her whole life that has culminated to this day which we all celebrate.

Hillary Clinton accepts the historic DNC nomination
and lends her voice and power to millions of others.
Photo: Fox61.com

From looking at Hillary Clinton's face you can surely
see the sadness in it as bears with the grieving woman.
That is what WETATians like her do.
Photo: Alobatnic.blog

Hillary Clinton knows when and how to lend her voice, influence and power where it really matters like making sure that after 9/11 the New York First Responders, the Veterans and others all received the much-needed support to begin restoration and healing; attentively listening to a Hispanic child's story about how fearful she is that her illegal parents may be deported to mentoring loads of girls, young women and many more without seeking public reward and adulation unless someone provokes the showing.

Photo: hillaryclinton.com

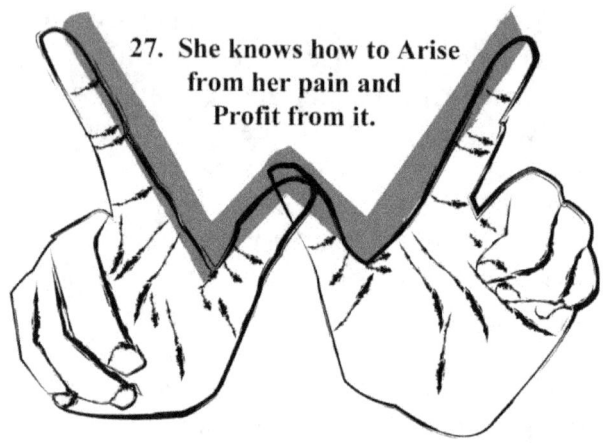

27. She knows how to Arise from her pain and Profit from it.

If anyone knows how to arise from pain, Hillary Clinton knows. That is why she is WETATi. If you have never fallen, you will never know how to stand solidly and profit from it. Hillary Clinton has had her own share of pain and has each time not only transcended, but transformed and profited from it while inspiring others. Only empowered people know how to do that, and when you are a WETATian you take it up a notch like Hillary Clinton has successfully done.

If you have the courage (bravery/ audacity) and strength (power/muscle) to survive (live to tell the tale/continue to exist)—YOU have the POWER (authority/

control) to SUCCEED (do well/achieve something/to thrive/to make it)—Restoration can only come if you know how to UNLEASH YOUR POWER WITHIN! This power exists in all of us...the difference in the result is how we go about unleashing it or not unleashing it and then creatively using it to restore, help others with it, and profit.

The essence of any pain in anyone's life is to profit oneself and to bless others with it, bring about change where possible, and not for the person to STORE it and die in silence.

Rest assured that if you have the courage to survive anything you have gone through or been through regardless of how it happened or who caused it, you have the power to succeed and live a better life than even before. Hillary Clinton knows this full well and has profited from it many times over.

It is very important to note that "we can't go back and make a brand new start, but we can from this point forward make a brand new ending." Also, to want what was, is another way of saying, "I don't want to grow up," because no one grows up meaningfully without going through. Without going through, you will never get through. Embrace your journey and learn how to arise from your pain and profit while using it to heal others along the way like Hillary Clinton. Leaders push through as WETATians do.

I believe that 'growing pain' is better than 'dying pain' because when you die it is over, but for as long as you are alive anything is POSSIBLE!

I DARE you to arise and find creative ways to profit from your pain, and somewhere along the line you will bless others with it which in most cases might have been the reason you went through the pain in the first place! Hillary Clinton is proof positive of that fact.

Hillary knows what it means to persevere, to be an overcomer, and to achieve success despite overwhelming odds and daunting challenges. Hillary is WETATi.

28. She knows that "impossibility is not a declaration; it's a dare."

As a WETATian, Hillary knows that impossibility is not simply an announcement (declaration) but a *taunt* (dare) to see if you will cave in and believe that it can't be done. Like a WETATian, Hillary knows that when people say that it is impossible to achieve, she sees it as a 'dare' or taunt instead, and that challenge provokes her to prove them wrong. She has done this all of her life and has almost always come out a winner because she is a woman who knows how to achieve the impossible and not only sees impossibility as a declaration but as a 'dare'. I believe that Hillary Clinton believes, from watching, researching and following her lifelong walk and work in how she conducts her businesses, that impossibility is simply a negative state of mind of those who don't want to go where others have never been before because they are afraid to be called hard names or even worse, to fail. Hillary understands that you can't succeed without being willing to fail, being vulnerable and embarrassed.

She has experienced it all and now stands to rule the world because she has earned it and didn't demand it. Like Walt Disney who said, "it's kind of fun to do the impossible."

Photo: Media.irishcentral.com

I believe Hillary Clinton, despite the negatives to the path she has chosen as a WETATi, thinks at some level like Walt Disney that it's fun to do the impossible. WETATians like to be dared, and they will prove you wrong. Hillary has proven them wrong as a WETATian.

29. She never gives up on her dreams and aspirations, no matter how long it may take to realize them.

Photo: Time.com

Hillary epitomizes this point in the sense that after she lost in 2008, hard and difficult as it was, she quietly moved on without much noise and waited another 8 years to try again. She never lost sight of what she was going for and why she was doing it. Here again, she understood what Lisa Abeyta meant when she said, "Yes, it may be necessary to fight for an opportunity, to struggle to break down a barrier to gain access to an opportunity. But stridence and friction will only get us so far. It is when we move beyond that struggle and change our mindset and become comfortable in our new role that we will have more confidence in ourselves and inspire it from others." Because at this point Hillary understood that she didn't have to operate with stridence and friction because she knows that she has moved beyond that struggle and has changed her mindset and become comfortable in her new role regarding what she deserves and has earned. At this point, she has stopped fighting for the opportunity and, instead, has stood up inside of that opportunity and owned it unapologetically. Like a true WETATian, she waited for the *change opportunity* that would not be fraught with so much friction and stridence. She also did a very noble thing which was going to work for the President, swallowing her ego to work with the person who had defeated her. That is priceless. This is what WETATians are made of.

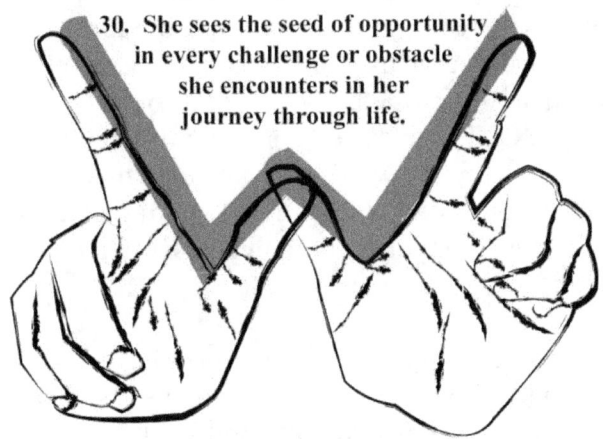

30. She sees the seed of opportunity in every challenge or obstacle she encounters in her journey through life.

In every adversity there is a SEED of opportunity if you know how to find it. Hillary knows how to turn *disappointments* into *divine appointment* like she did when she lost to President Obama in 2008. That is what WETATians do.

When something happens to you, you have just two choices. One: Do you let that define you and become a negative stronghold on your life? Or, Two: Do you accept what happened and use it as a catalyst to launch or catapult you to the *new normal* which often will give you the life that you never even knew was possible with your old normalcy?

What you choose to see or take away from the adversity which is inevitable for everyone as long as you are on earth, is what will determine whether you 'got it' or 'it GOT YOU!' A close examination of Hillary Clinton's life and work will elucidate this fact that she definitely knows how to extrapolate the seeds of opportunity in every adversity she has been through.

As an African woman leader, I have watched Hillary Clinton go through so many unbearable things in her life and work but have never seen her give up or complain publicly no matter what type of mud people throw at her. At times when I'm going through my own life and work challenges, I reference how she handles and goes through hers with grace, quiet confidence, dignity, poise and almost immediately flips it around like nothing just happened. Hillary, like a true WETATian, knows that disappointment is a boundless propellant to greatness if you know how to use it. Hillary Clinton is WETATi.

31. SHE KNOWS THAT IT IS IMPORTANT TO SUPPORT OTHERS EVEN IF IT IS NOT EXPEDIENT.

I've noted from outside looking in, from research, information and observation, Hillary Clinton seems to be motivated and moved by other people's needs or pain. She doesn't seem to do something because it is expedient but because it is the right thing to do for the people and as a public servant. The testament of this aspect of her life came to bear during the historic Democratic National Convention when a slew of people showed up to testify how she has impacted them, and I am sure there is much more to tell. That is why she is WETATi.

I believe that people should support others because it is the right thing to do even if they see no apparent reason to do so. God will reward you even if you do not believe in God. Support others when you can, because you never know how things will turn around and you will need them too. Support others even if you cannot relate to their problems. Support others in their causes even when you do not believe in what they might have done, because the *essence of support* should be because you realize that people in need are God's children regardless of what they might have done. Supporting someone is not necessarily condoning what the person did or agreeing with what they did, what they want or are in need of.

Supporting someone in times of hardship or adversity may be what will change that person's life for that time, or for life. I will let you in on a secret: If you do not support someone in need, God will support that person in ways you would not believe and then you will say, "I wish I had supported him or her." Support is love and love is God, and with God everything is possible. In this regard, I always recall the wise saying, **"never be afraid to entertain strangers because some have entertained angels unaware." For those who support halfway and quit, it is a very dangerous thing to do; the person you just gave up on may not** survive it, because they could have been relying on you to keep on going. Sometimes, haphazard support is more damaging than not giving any support at all. Incomplete support of any kind can be a very dangerous and devastating thing for the person receiving it.

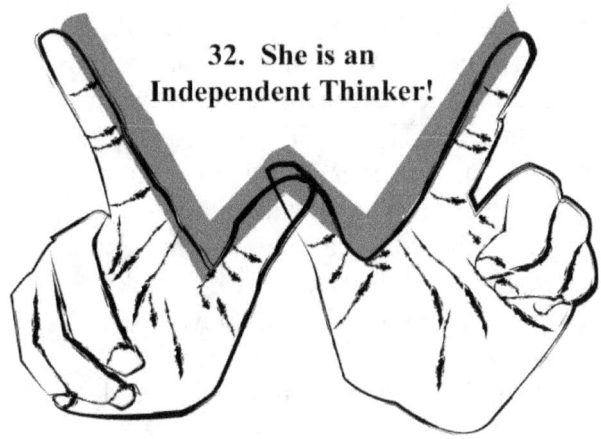

32. She is an Independent Thinker!

Hillary is a WETATi woman because she is an independent thinker. "To be independent of public opinion is the very first condition to achieving anything great." To be independent of public opinion is the very first condition if one is to live authentically.

Walt Disney was once told that he could not make a living as an artist, and his answer was—

"I will try." The rest is history! By the same token, Hillary Clinton was told by many pundits that she couldn't achieve becoming a nominee of a major political party in America, and she ignored them and did just that as a WETATi woman and is on her way to becoming the next historic first woman President of the United States of America. As a WETATian and as an African woman leader I have been told by many and whispered about by many more that I could not achieve what I set out to do, and like Hillary I ignored them and achieved it.

The point is that it is not what people say we can't do that stops us, it is what WE say we cannot do. Walt Disney believed in himself and his abilities; all we need to do is believe in ourselves and 'go for it' like Walt and Hillary Clinton.

Right or Independent Thinking + Right products/service + right person(s) = success!

How many 'Walts' do we have out there who are afraid to fight to be FREE creatively

and actually do something about it like
Hillary Clinton, and stay the course to see it
come to fruition? Hillary is WETATi.

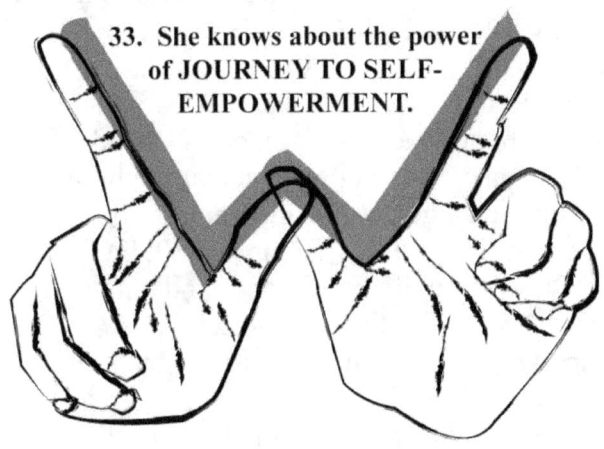

33. She knows about the power
of **JOURNEY TO SELF-
EMPOWERMENT.**

To me, **Empowerment** really means to
fuel or energize self, someone else or groups
of people with a common goal or purpose, to
believe that one's objectives or goals can be
accomplished with a *positive mental attitude*
and *strong faith in oneself and in one's
creator.* It can also mean to gain a new
insight or perspective on how one can do
things which were previously thought
impossible. It can also mean acquiring a new
vision or insight on how to actualize self or
realize one's full potential despite all the odds
against them. Empowerment also equips one

to dare to take the 'road less traveled' to find one's purpose in life and to make a difference in the lives of others. You can't be self-empowered if you don't have a very strong sense of self. Hillary Clinton's journey to self-empowerment is evident as she has managed to weave a life that most would only dream about which started when she made the realization as a young woman that she has the power to change her life and impact others along the way. Hillary Clinton is WETATi because she totally understands and knows about the power of journey to self-empowerment. When you examine the life and walk of a WETATian like Clinton, you can see the evidence from the fruits of their work and walk in life.

When empowerment is acquired, coupled with aspiration, inspiration and one's core beliefs, it can really move mountains. When self-empowerment is obtained, the **impossible** becomes **possible** and the **"I can't do's"** become **"I can do's"**. It restores one's self-esteem, self-confidence and self-worth irrespective of how others may perceive one's actions or views on things. When self-empowerment is achieved or restored, your "no" is your "no" and your "yes" is your "yes". It is when you know who you are and become very sure of yourself. ***When self-empowerment is acquired, one is able to <u>turn adversities</u> into <u>blessings and stepping stones.</u>***

To find empowerment, one must reach deep down into one's body, mind, spirit and soul. There are lots of contributing factors that affect the quality and quantity of one's sources of empowerment. One's place of birth, family upbringing, environmental conditions during developmental stages of a child leading to adulthood, and peer pressure are some of the factors. Other factors are one's socio-economic status, one's significant others' influences, churches, religious beliefs, one's circle of friends and a person's natural dispositions towards empowerment.

However, the bottom line lies in the **belief systems** of the individual and their **faith in God**. Some empowerment comes from the **remnants** of the adversities of life that strengthen one's character. Empowerment is very crucial to the successes that one achieves in life. Whether success is in the home front, business or any other, it often derives input from that individual's empowerment beliefs. One can never achieve anything constructive and fulfilling in one's life in the absence of empowerment, inspiration, desire, and strong faith in God. Empowerment is one characteristic of humans that every single person **must possess** in order to **succeed in today's world**. One should never give their empowerment up for any reason, even when the very core of their being is threatened. When in doubt, just think about the "Mr. Hurricane" movie that was actually based on a true story. Now, that is one self-empowered young man who, even in the face of losing his physical freedom and possibly his life, he held on to his power. Had Mr. Hurricane surrendered his power, he definitely could not have survived his nineteen years of imprisonment for something he did not even do. A person who has lost their willpower or self-empowerment has lost the essence of his or her being and that which defines who and what he or she is and stands for.

As they say, "when you do not stand for something, you will fall for anything." Basically, when you give up power, you give up your decision-making abilities and that which makes you human, and other people then decide for you. At that point, you are only getting the crumbs of the powerful. I sincerely believe that people who often complain about things which **they can do something about** are those who have *passively* or *actively, knowingly or unknowingly,* given up their *power (intentionally or unintentionally).*

Those who have given up power are those who often have also given up hope in life and have lost belief in themselves, and now depend on what other people expect of them. Though, at times it is not obvious that some who give up their power really realize that this is what has happened. Sometimes, it is so subtle that they will not even realize it. Therefore, one must always take time to *reflect* and *re-evaluate* any circumstances one finds him/herself in over time.

Whatever you do, you must gain your freedom through self-empowerment at <u>any price</u> because that is who you are. This power that I am alluding to here is not the one you <u>exert</u> over other people in an unconscionable way or that exists in a master-servant relationship. It is the power that <u>exists in all of us</u> that some choose to ignore or <u>relinquish</u> to others. The power is freedom from servitude, poverty, and a shackled spirit. It's the freedom to be your own boss, to marry or not to marry, etc. It's

**the freedom to do whatever you want to do
but against no one.**

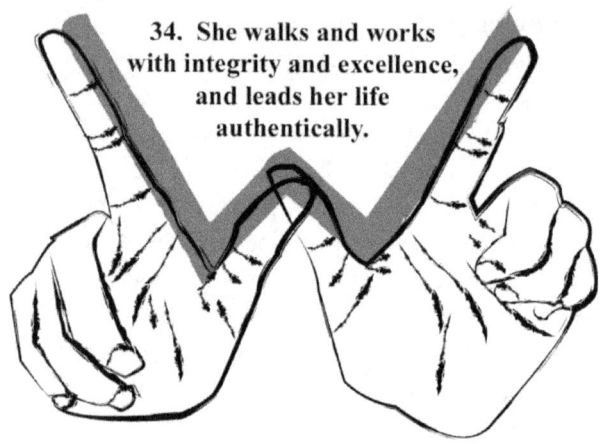

**34. She walks and works
with integrity and excellence,
and leads her life
authentically.**

To walk and work with integrity and
excellence and lead your life authentically,
you must be consistent in character like
Hillary Clinton.

Consistency produces integrity. To be a
consistent person requires that you stand for
something which over time will define you as
a person of integrity or the reverse. To
become someone of integrity, you must begin
to "dig your well before you are thirsty"
because you cannot just wake up one day and
ask others to see you as such. If you have
never treated others the way you would like

to be treated and you say one thing and do the other, it means that you are living as a hypocrite and in time it will become clear who you really are and the fruit of what you have sown will be right there looking at you, and now there will be no escape.

A consistent character is the one who is the same person in their private life as they are in public. Without living a life of integrity, it is virtually impossible to attain a fulfilling and meaningful place in life. When you are consistent, you have a different mindset from the lot and you don't have to seek to be successful. All you need to do is live a life of significance, and success will beget you. Integrity calls for doing what is right even when no one is watching. Hillary Clinton is WETATi because she works and walks with integrity.

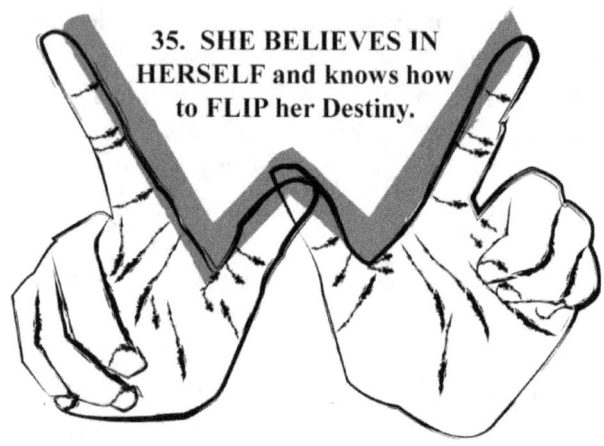

35. SHE BELIEVES IN HERSELF and knows how to FLIP her Destiny.

Hillary Clinton is WETATi because she believes in herself and knows how to flip her destiny each and every time her destiny is challenged. To believe in yourself is to not be rattled by anything or by anyone no matter what happens or doesn't happen. To believe in yourself is to know who you are and whose you are no matter what the circumstance may APPEAR to be at the time.

When you believe in yourself, NOTHING can SHIFT you out of your element and cause you to lose momentum and focus. When you believe in yourself, you know - that you know - that you know why. When you believe in yourself, indecision and doubt will not be your portion. When you believe in yourself, you are very assured of your BEING and DOING, and you are very confident of yourself without being arrogant about it; you make no apologies for what you believe and the choices you have made and will make.

When you believe in yourself, you will not be all things to all people, and you stand for what you believe in no matter what others say or think about it; you will not seek approval from others because you have already accepted and approved yourself.

When you believe in yourself, magic happens. When you believe in yourself, doors begin to open wider than before, acceptance magnifies and your sense of self-worth heightens, and your sense of purpose and direction are exponential in magnitude all around.

To believe in yourself is to believe in the God who created you, and at that point nothing else matters because God is the only ONE who can truly CHANGE YOUR COURSE THE WAY NO MAN CAN!

If you don't believe in yourself, no one else will. Hillary Clinton believes in herself, looks ahead and understands that what is ahead is far greater than what is behind. As a visionary leader and WETATian Hillary knows that she must be assertive and yet humble and optimistic.

Because she BELIEVES IN HERSELF AND OWNS IT, difficult doors begin to open without ceasing!

36. She Doesn't Believe It!

What you believe is KEY to what you become and what you do and how you live.

When life presents or gives you what is inconsistent with what God wants for you— don't believe it. When the people around say something about you that is not TRUE, no

matter how many times they say it to you—
don't believe it. Clue: stay away from them
and move toward LIGHT!

Your belief system is KEY to whether or
not you become successful in life and
business. So, when people tell you that your
business idea or dream to do something
bigger than yourself is not possible—don't
believe them. When people tell you that you
are up to no good because they don't believe
in your dream or even worse refuse to support
you—don't believe it (realize that at times
they tell you that because they can't do what
you can do, and rather than encourage you,
they try to pull you down with their PhD's
(pull her or pull him down degrees). Don't
believe it!

When you believe BIG and "they" say
you are crazy—don't believe it because most
"normal" people never achieve beyond the
norm. Believe in yourself and continue to
press forward because in time "they" will
come to learn from you and join you because
you defied their naysaying.

Don't believe it when they tell you that
you will never make it in school or at
anything else for that matter—don't believe it

because if you believe in yourself and the God who created you and gave power to create, you can achieve anything you put your mind to as long as you have the mind to do it, you find and stay with people who will support and encourage your talents and ambitions, and you are willing to endure to the end.

Don't believe that because no one knows your name, you will not make it—don't believe it. If God is for you, no one can be against you.

All power belongs to Jesus and because you have God in you, you have power. Don't believe that anyone else is better than you, because they are not unless you allow their idiosyncrasies to influence your MIND and your THINKING and you then begin to think less of yourself—remember that no one can intimidate you unless you give into it or allow it. It is a mindset thing—be mindful of it daily. Hillary Clinton is well aware of this and does not believe any negative sayings about her by anyone because she truly knows who she is and what she stands for. That is why Hillary is a full-fledged WETATian.

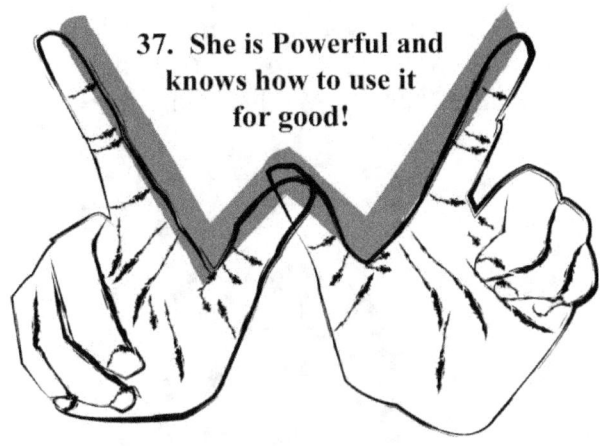

37. She is Powerful and knows how to use it for good!

A WETATi woman is powerful, but how she chooses to use that power is what differentiates her from others. Hillary Clinton is powerful, and how she uses it as a mother, grandmother, wife and Presidential aspirant is what women leaders like me who have been watching her intently and admiringly are impressed by. To have power is not powerful. What is powerful is how you choose to exert power with those under your command.

To exert power over others just because you can is the WEAKEST form of exerting power and brings the weakest wimp to power unbeknownst to you. Through research and information, we have seen how quietly and gently Clinton exerts her power even when no one is watching by treating others the way she would like to be treated. That and much more qualifies her as a WETATian.

Hillary Clinton giving speech for the Arkansas Children's Hospital
Photo: clinton3.nara.gov

Photo: zimbio.com

The next time you want to wield your power just because you are in a position of authority, remember that you are the weakest. Hillary Clinton knows this inverted form of power and uses it effectively to touch lives positively.

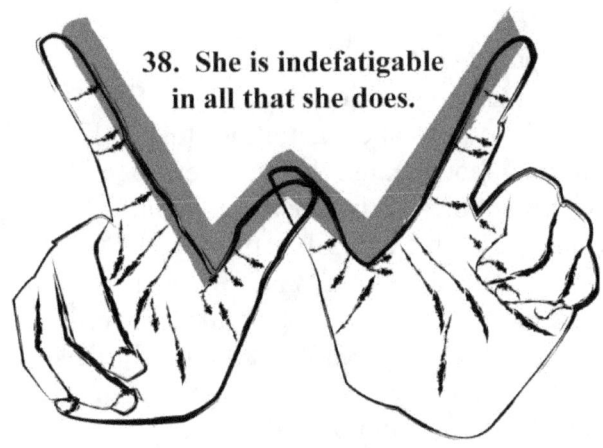

38. She is indefatigable in all that she does.

Hillary is WETATi because she is indefatigable. **To be indefatigable is to be successful!**

To be indefatigable is to be tireless in the pursuit of your life's ambition and purpose in the face of all obstacles, challenges and adversities, and without losing focus and hope that the end will justify the means and without feeling despondent and hopeless during the journey.

It does not matter how many times you have failed or tried. Hillary Clinton has never relented in her pursuit and has been courageous in the face of it.

Courage is Grace under pressure. Without Grace your journey through life would be odious and frustrating. Just realize that you labor because you are blessed, and you are not blessed because you labor. Hillary Clinton exemplifies this very important attribute of a WETATi woman and much more. As an African woman leader it resonates with me because at my level I have experienced most of what she has though from a different context.

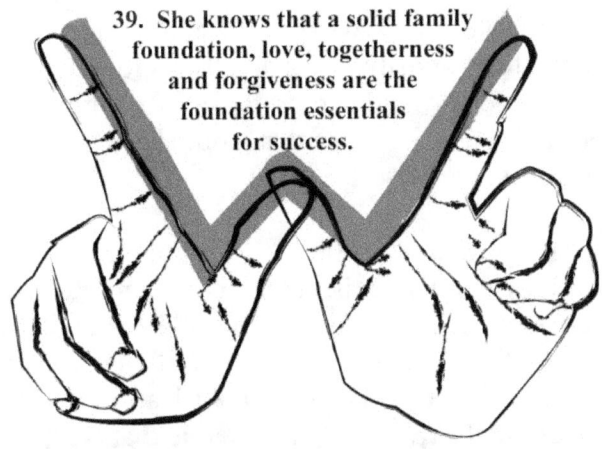

39. She knows that a solid family foundation, love, togetherness and forgiveness are the foundation essentials for success.

Photo: CNN.com

Yes, of course everyone knows that Hillary has had many marital issues with her spouse, and because she is in the public eye, it's magnified beyond what it would have been for average folks. I guess that proves that she is human like the rest of us, but what

123

is admirable is how without ceasing she has always found positive, creative ways to turn the situation around and protect and restore her family despite those that would have preferred otherwise.

What kind of problems do you have, and how do you resolve them? I am not here to endorse or discredit Hillary, because I am not in a position to do so nor am I qualified or in her shoes to do so. There is an African proverb that says, "it's only the one that is wearing the shoe that knows exactly where the corn on her feet hurts." However, I am stating that Hillary is WETATi because WETATi women handle their affairs with much more poise and order. Yes, she has had conflicts in her marriage, but she didn't let it destroy them.

The functions of conflict in a marriage should be to __strengthen__ the relationship and bring the couple __closer than before__ not distance them. This result will only come about if you __know how__ to fight as a couple. *It is not what the fight is about that matters; it is **how you __choose__ to resolve it**.* If you choose badly, you may fall victim to divorce or be like many who stay in the institution of marriage just to pretend to the world that they are, Mrs. Somebody.

This is one of the most serious atrocities a person can commit against him or herself. The reason is because you owe it to yourself never to live a life of lies, deception and un-fulfillment just to make believe. It is really how you resolve the conflict that makes the difference and not what caused the conflict in the first place.

Hillary's and Bill's divine bond defies all odds.
Photo: wnd.com

When couples learn to celebrate their "differences" instead of their "similarities", then and only then will they really enjoy each other's special gifts from God.

Photo: Deadline.com

40. She knows The Power of Change and why We Need Change.

What is change? Change is a necessary force in life which if utilized properly, can be therapeutic to the body, mind, and spirit. Change can also result in a turning point that you did not know you needed. So do not resist change. Hillary Clinton as a WETATian does not resist change.

Change can become a very positive force in one's life depending on the response one gives it. In saying this, I am not attempting to minimize the impact and the instant trauma change can cause in people's lives whenever, however and wherever it occurs. However, if you p**erceive** and **receive** change with a **positive mental attitude**, you are sure to come out of it a **winner** and become a <u>**victor**</u> like Hillary Clinton instead of a **victim**.

Ever since I changed **how** I perceive changes in my life, I am much happier and can adapt to a new situation with a healthier mental attitude. I do not want it to sound like this is an easy task to do either. It also acts as a propellant to people's motivation to act rather than react. However, *nothing worth having is easy to come by*. **So get over it, face life head on, call it no bad or hard names and you will see how much lighter and humorous life's burdens will feel.** We need change because it is about the only thing that really seems to make people take action and responsibility or take control of things.

There will never be change without change, there will never be change without challenge, and definitely there will never be change without sacrifice. In some cases, some people's most fulfilling work or worthy courses come about from change or challenge. Hillary is WETATi because she is a change agent.

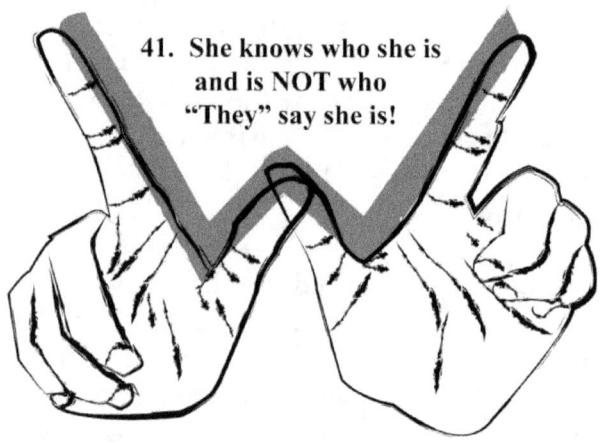

41. She knows who she is and is NOT who "They" say she is!

Hillary is WETATi because WETATians unequivocally know who they are regardless of what others say they are. What people call you is irrelevant. It is what you answer to that matters. You are who you say you are by the way you live and conduct your life and business daily.

You are not who others say you are by the way they perceive you. The only way you will be the person others say you are is by doing and being what their projection of you is.

However, when you have the audacity to be and do YOU the ONLY way you know how, they will bow down and marvel at how awesome your God is! You have nothing to prove to anyone but everything to prove to yourself; by default "they" will submit to your unflinching power and success.

Hillary completely embraces who she has been created to be and makes no apologies for who she is. Anyone paying close attention to this presidential campaign knows exactly what I mean by that because there is no name in the book that she hasn't been called, but despite it all she perseveres because she knows full well that it is not what they call her but what she answers to. She also knows to be a WETATian, those types of misconceptions come along with the territory.

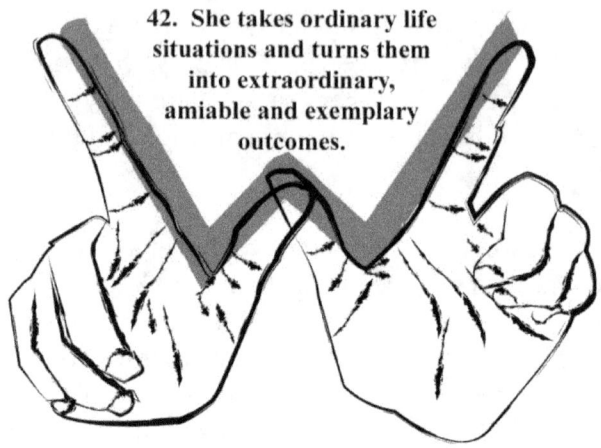

42. She takes ordinary life situations and turns them into extraordinary, amiable and exemplary outcomes.

Hillary knows that you don't discover success; you stumble upon it by doing what you have never done before with intention, passion, strategy, game plan; and seeking to live a life of significance and on purpose...no matter the cost.

Hillary knows how to turn every disadvantage into an advantage; her whole life and profession are marked with those facts, and that is one of the reasons she is WETATi. She knows how to turn ordinary into extraordinary. She is simplistic by nature and not apt to try to impress people by **making believe** she's a brand that she is not.

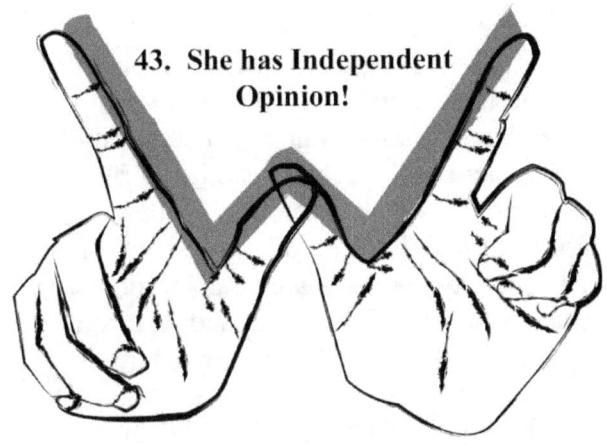

43. She has Independent Opinion!

Hillary is WETATi because she is independent of other people's opinion of her. However, she takes counsel when and where needed. To be independent of other people's opinion is the very first condition to knowing who you are, what you stand for and what you want to do with your life without fainting because of what others think of you.

Inferiority complex is a state of mind, and no one can infiltrate your mindset unless you allow them to regardless of the circumstances at the time. Independent thinkers are radicals who will lay everything down for what they believe in and will fight for the sake of others.

Independent thinkers are often not appreciated by the majority because the majorities are often in the lane of "that is OK" and "everything is going to be all right," when in fact nothing is going to be all right unless you do something about it. The majority of people want to be loved and/or liked. The independents are goal/solution-to-problem oriented. To be independent of other people's opinions is to have the audacity to be you—no matter what or before whom. They are the FREEDOM fighters. They are not the COMPLAINERS of what is wrong. They don't have time to gossip. They are constructive in their engagements. Hillary Clinton is an independent thinker, sound and solid in her opinions.

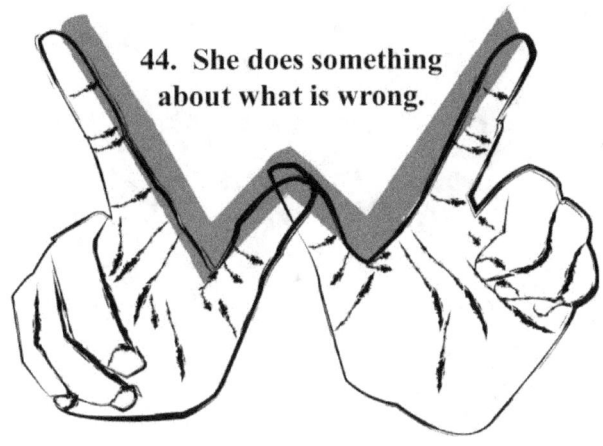

44. She does something about what is wrong.

Hillary is WETATi because she knows how to do something about what is wrong and not just sit and criticize or complain without action. She is a successful fighter and knows how to fight for others as has been testified to by a multitude of people.

Hillary Clinton "Fighting for us." *Photo: 5newsonline.com*

45. She knows that her faith in God is her compass in her journey through life.

Prayer is the vehicle you use to call faith and action into being. Prayer can stop any storm coming against you no matter how formidable it may seem. Prayer can take care of all the worries you have about your day, your abilities or inabilities to overcome life's challenges, your insecurities and much more.

When prayer does not stop the onslaught of whatever it may be, it will give you the GRACE to go through and get through it in peace and not in pieces. Remember that to go through is to get through. If you don't go through, you will never get through. As a WETATian Hillary Clinton gets this because she knows how to use her faith as a compass to navigate her journey through life.

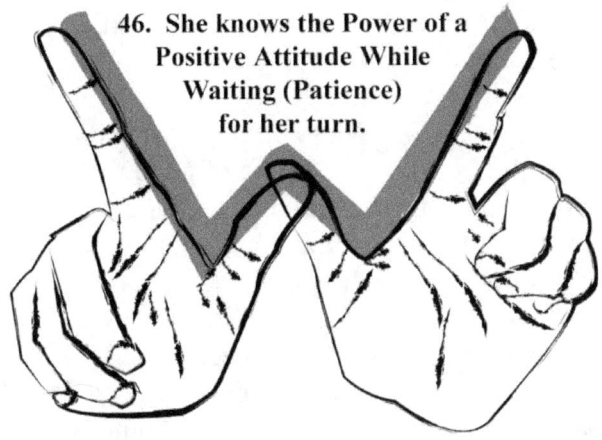

46. She knows the Power of a Positive Attitude While Waiting (Patience) for her turn.

Hillary Clinton definitely knows the power and importance of a positive attitude while waiting and to never let her enemies see her sweat, like other WETATians around the world.

A positive attitude enabled me to accomplish the impossible.

A positive attitude under any circumstance never fails no matter how bleak the condition may be or seem. It has been established that those who have a positive attitude toward life tend to rebound after adversity. A positive attitude while you wait for things to turn around for you will determine the degree of patience you exude while going through a trying time.

Psalm 27:14, "Wait and hope for and expect the Lord; be brave and of good courage and let your heart be stout and enduring. Yes, wait for and hope for and expect the Lord," is literally talking about "patience". Waiting does not literally mean doing nothing. It means you become a prisoner of hope and indefatigable toward the goal until you get home whatever "home" may be for you in your situation.

The key words to indicate that this verse is talking about having active patience are: "wait", "hope", "enduring", and "expect".

A Positive Attitude in the midst of the storm or journey makes all the difference in the outcome—no matter what the situation may be. Negativism will never generate positivity, unless you turn a negative event into a positive one. Resist the urge to be negative, because it will never work in your favor!

Your mental attitude will determine the altitude you will get in life. Hillary epitomizes this fact and that is why she is WETATi.

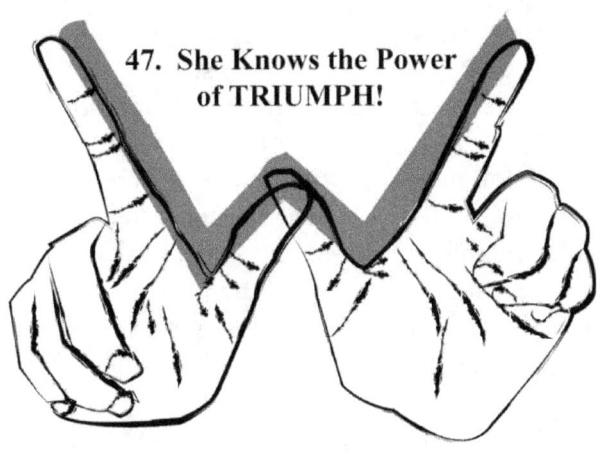

47. She Knows the Power of TRIUMPH!

Success or power cannot be obtained and sustained until **consistency** and **SELF** are mastered. Triumph simply means victory. Triumph or victory is experienced when you are consistent and sure in all your ways of being and doing. You cannot be triumphant with your dreams and goals until you align them 100% with your passion, purpose, values, and core beliefs which in turn creates the success desired. 0.1% doubt you are out—PERIOD!

Romans 8:29-39, "…we are more than conquerors through Him." When you are consistent, prayerful and determined, you are able to stand the test of time, because we are more than conquerors. You cannot be triumphant without a test. You cannot testify without a test. You cannot minister IMPACTFULLY where you have not bled.

A conquering spirit enables you to endure to finally experience success that is only available for those who know how to stick and stay until they get their rewards and not be in too much of a hurry to get to the finish line or to get to nowhere.

This finish line is really promised to each and every one of us because God is no respecter of persons; what He does for one He can do for another, but first we must meet the conditions to partake and be steadfast or consistent which is one of the elements required.

The power of triumph is the victory or the wonderful feeling of exhilaration you feel and release when you achieve against all the odds along the way. Hillary Clinton definitely knows about it. Only those who are consistent and determined will experience this triumphant phenomenon.

The Power of Triumph is the power to achieve your goals and ambitions against all odds, on your own terms, and at your own pace and not within anyone else's prescription or ascription of what triumph may look like. Hillary Clinton is a triumphant WETATi.

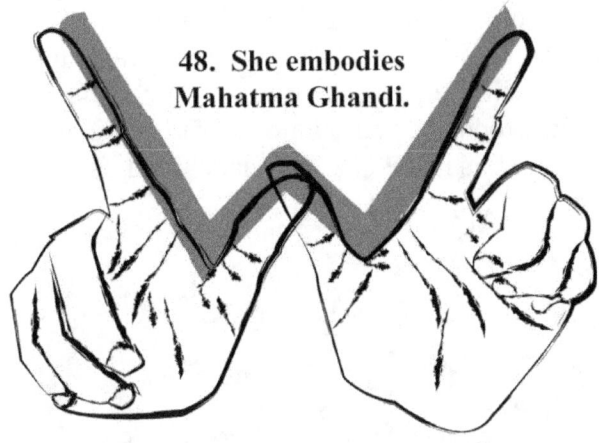

48. She embodies Mahatma Ghandi.

Hillary Clinton is WETATi because she embodies the spirit of Mahatma Gandhi. She personifies Mahatma Gandhi's philosophy of life and business which has helped me to shape my own life and career against all the odds that I have faced.

Mahatma Gandhi and his life philosophy is definitely one that I can point to which has

139

helped me in difficult places of my life when people around me simply don't have the answer. Through him I discovered that when you are a visionary, if you stay with non-visionaries, your vision will die. Gandhi's philosophy empowered and changed mine and taught me what I should strive to be and not follow just for the sake of expediency, or even worse so that "they" would approve. His philosophy is for anyone who really wants to make a difference in the lives of others and not just focus on self. Out of all of his wise sayings, this is the one that made the most profound impact on me.

Mahatma Gandhi
Photo: Rocksea.org

(1) **"First they ignore you."** I have learned over the years that when the strength in you brings out the weakness in others, they will hate you for it. They immediately devise a conspiratorial attitude of avoidance and ignore you which, if you are not mindful or sure of yourself and your stand in life, you would think you might have done something to them which now comes from them ignoring you in more ways than one.

A WETATian knows that it is not her, but the distinctive (Eagle) in her has provoked the jealousy (chicken) in them that now touches a chord with their insecurities, and one of the signs of that from the chickens is "let's ignore her;" which in my book is yet another source of inspiration to press on further and stronger than ever before because I know that there is nothing there. An important point to mention is that though they want you to believe that they have ignored you, the truth of the matter is that they are still secretly checking you out and wondering how you are doing it.

(2) **"Then they laugh at you."** If you have never been laughed at, you have never achieved the impossible. Normally, when you start to go where others haven't gone before,

the tendency for those around you (many of whom are not doing anything of distinction) is to start laughing at you and labeling you. A WETATian knows when this is going on and ignores those laughing at her and presses forward. Hillary Clinton is a WETATian because she has been laughed at many times but she ignores them and keeps pressing forward toward the mark.

(3) **"Then they fight you."** The fight phase of Mahatma Gandhi's philosophy on how to ignore the naysayers as a visionary when you are moving toward an unusual calling like Hillary Clinton, is that after they ignore you when you first state your intention to achieve the impossible in whatever field it is, they fight you to see if they can distract you from following through with your vision.

As a WETATian, Hillary Clinton immediately understands what is going on as the second phase of Gandhi's premise and rather than react to the distractions, which is often full of empty noises, she keeps the faith toward the mark and stays determined more than ever to prove them wrong. If no one is fighting you, you are not doing anything of landmark proportions. A WETATian knows that the "can'ts" cannot be where the "cans" are.

(4) **and "then YOU WIN!"** The fourth part of this principle of Gandhi is knowing that after they fight you, then you WIN, and this is the beauty of it all. It's like letting you know that there is a reward in the end if you stay the course. A WETATian understands this and therefore does not get off focus during phases 1, 2 and 3 because she knows that the end is near and triumph will always trump the agonies of the other parts. I am confident that Hillary Clinton has experienced all four of these attributes. When she first made it public that she aspired to run for the highest office in the world—the presidency of the United States of America— many ignored her in hopes she would go away or even worse thought that she must have lost her mind. But a WETATi woman is at her best when she is dared by the naysayers. A WETATian is not bothered by the negative name calling of the haters and/or those who do not want them to come up higher, because a WETATi woman always knows who she is even in the midst of the storm and daunting obstacles and challenges like Hillary Clinton has demonstrated throughout her life and career.

It is hopefully common knowledge that if you haven't been laughed at, you have not dared to achieve anything worthwhile. Every WETATi woman knows when they are doing something that most would say "not for me," their strength will bring out the weakness in others and they will hate you for it or start calling you hard names.

49. She doesn't worry if people don't understand her!

Hillary is WETATi because she doesn't worry if people don't understand her. She does the **very best she can and keeps moving her agenda toward the goal**.

Don't worry if people don't understand you or they misunderstand you. What you should worry about is if you don't understand

YOURSELF or even worse, if you misunderstand yourself. To understand yourself is to be sure of who you are, what you stand for, whose you are and where you are going; and you will not flinch when others misunderstand you because you are coming from a different place that they would never UNDERSTAND! That right there is POWER!

50. She knows that ONE SEASON prepares for the NEXT SEASON; and She MAKES HARD CHOICES.

Photo: Upi.com

Hillary is WETATi because she makes hard choices. "Secretary Clinton and President Obama had to decide how to repair fractured alliances, wind down two wars, and address a global financial crisis. Along the way, they grappled with tough dilemmas,

146

especially the decision to send Americans
into harm's way, from Afghanistan to Libya
to the hunt for Osama bin Laden. By the end
of her tenure, Secretary Clinton had gained a
truly global perspective on the major trends
reshaping today's landscape." – By Hillary
Clinton on her book, *"Hard Choices"*.

Photo: Charlotteobserver.com

Never resent any season that you are in
because that is part of your journey and part
of the ingredients necessary in rough-hewing
the formidable person that you will become
tomorrow. That season prepares you for the
next one! Embrace! Accept! Innovate! Grow!
Impact!

51. She is comfortable around
other strong women and
equally celebrates
their successes.

From one WETATian to another, and confident in their
individual powers; Hillary Clinton and Madeleine Albright.
AP Photo: Stephan Savoia

Photo: Multimedia.blogosfere.it

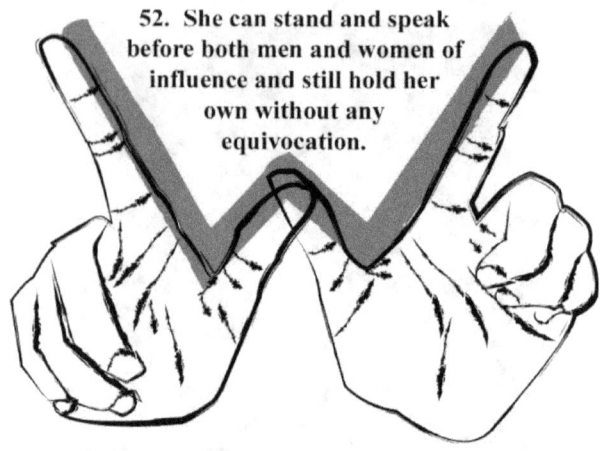

52. She can stand and speak before both men and women of influence and still hold her own without any equivocation.

Photo:i.ytimg.com

Hillary is WETATi because she possesses these exceptional qualities that are the main yardsticks for WETATians all over the world. The only difference may be that for one woman it may be running for the highest office in the world, and for some it may be pushing and fighting hard to make sure their children go to school, as they themselves may never have been successful in completing school.

As an African woman leader, watching Hillary Clinton do this time and again despite the hard names people call her, I know that I can do that too and succeed despite the hard names people call me.

Photo: Media2.today.in

Amongst the men, she stood her ground with poise, intelligence, dignity and power.

Even while standing between men of power with sharp cultural
differences, Hillary stands her ground. – #WETATipower
Photo: Img.antaranews.com

Diplomacy is in her DNA and she knows
that Conflict destroys concentration and
productivity!

It is virtually impossible to concentrate
and get anything meaningful while in
conflict. Though conflict is inevitable
sometimes, you must understand that in order
to concentrate and accomplish, you must
AVOID conflict at all cost.

Remember that discovering the essence
of CONFLICT is to sort out what is wrong or
what is not agreed upon by two or more
people or by a group.

Constructive conflict is to solve a problem or misunderstanding and it not be dragged out for so long that it loses its essence. This is often one of the reasons most wars in the world are prolonged for years without ending, because a conflict that was to be resolved was prolonged to the extent that after a time, no one can even remember why they were fighting in the first place, but yet they feel compelled to continue to fight.

Without concentration you cannot focus, and without focus you cannot create on purpose and achieve your target.

Instead of fighting to destroy, why can't people fight to BUILD? There are more benefits to fighting to build than fighting to destroy. Most people would rather destroy than build (I never understand that).

I avoid unnecessary "drama" or conflict like a plague, but I FIGHT for what I believe in as if my life depends on it because it does. There is a big difference between the two.

Fight to BUILD and NOT to DESTROY! There are more destroyers in the world than builders; which one are you?

There is no power in engaging in negative conflict, but there is a lot of power in temporary constructive conflict to make a point and to bring about change and not just to exert power just because you can or just because you have nothing better to do than cause conflict everywhere you go.

Conflicts destroy concentration and productivity, so CHOOSE your fights WISELY.

Hillary is WETATi because she knows that conflict destroys concentration, and so she does everything she can to make sure to avoid negative conflict.

Hillary is WETATi and today and henceforth, on behalf of all African women and others elsewhere, I have the privilege and honor to crown Hillary Clinton as a WETATian and warn that no one should ever underestimate the power of a WETATi woman because they can be and achieve anything they put their minds to. They can achieve the impossible. Hillary Clinton is proof positive of that despite those who said it can't be done.

Letter to Madam President Hillary Clinton

RE: *Africans' Needs and Lives Matter*

On behalf of Africans in America, and on behalf of WETATi women around the globe and African women in particular, I would like to say CONGRATULATIONS on this momentous achievement.

The reason for this letter is to beg of you that you should not forget Africans in your administration like others have, as our needs and lives matter too. The truth of the matter is that a very small number of Africans have been utilized during political seasons and given little tokens to make them believe that they are part of the process which in no way or form reflects the totality of the dire circumstances of our true and real struggles in America as a people that have gone unnoticed and unattended to for decades.

Africans in America have been disenfranchised, disillusioned, disrespected, ignored, maltreated and rejected to name a few issues, for so long that it kind of seems and feels normal now when we should feel that it's an atrocity because it is simply inhumane. But again I can understand how that could be because it is not easy for sojourners in a foreign land who are the first generations to go through this kind of situation.

However, because of the faith I have in the American system and its ways of doing things, I believe when the time is right, Africans and their needs and rights will matter. That time has come because as a woman, I believe you will 'get it' more than anyone else. I know for a fact that in America when any injustice is exposed and called into question and brought to the attention of the right authorities, more often than not something will be done about it.

At times it seems like Africans do not have a stake in the issues that matter to all. At times it feels like nobody cares about us or that our needs are irrelevant. At times we don't even know whether or not we belong as no one ever mentions us when and where it matters in the system. Are we part of the system? I really can't answer that confidently in the affirmative because the majority of times it doesn't feel or seem that way.

Please Madam President, Hillary Clinton, help Africans as our lives and needs matter too though I still see myself as American having lived here for over 30 years. America is now our home, but by the way we are treated the majority of times, we are constantly reminded that it may not be, or is it? Our struggles are unique to us and I think anyone who hasn't been through what we have been through cannot even begin to fathom what that feels like; however, empathetically thinking one can imagine, and if we are each other's keeper, all lives MUST MATTER because we are all God's children doing our individual bests with what we are given, with the opportunities we have been able to create or find; after all, this is the United States of America.

There are millions of Africans in America who matter during political seasons, but they manage to dissipate right after. This cannot be right, though some of us have resigned and taken it as the way things are; but I DARE to question it because America has given me the audacity to do so but in good faith, good conscience and with no malice.

Madam President Hillary Clinton, my prayer and hope is that when you take office you will not forget Africans, our needs and voices. We are very hard working, contributing members of the community and this great nation. At times, some of us feel like outcasts as we fade into thin air when and where it really matters.

Madam President Hillary Clinton, from a fellow WETATi woman to another, I am confident that your administration will give Africans in America the equal opportunities we deserve like others. I believe things could be different under your administration because for one, women are more attentive to details, instinctive to others' feelings and needs, and more caring and compassionate. I also believe that you, especially at this time in our lives and history, will understand and be willing to do something about it if you can. I believe that you can, despite the realistic expected oppositions you may face when you dare to look in our direction and attempt to do something about our unfair situations.

Knowing that you are not afraid to go where others have not gone before or dare to go, I believe in my heart that you will do the RIGHT thing if it's brought to your attention. As an African woman leader and as a fellow WETATian, I believe that though we have been disenfranchised and marginalized for decades, it's never too late to RIGHT THE WRONGS of our past by doing the right things going forward, and as a progressive-minded president, I believe you will bring change and make a difference in our current plights in America!

On behalf of Africans in America, we say congratulations. May God Almighty protect and guide you as you begin a big and bright chapter in your life and career.

WETATifully Yours,

Ambassador Dr. Margaret Dureke
Founder and President of WETATi
& margaretspeaks.com

Anne Reese Carswell, The Associate Director of Nyumburu Cultural Center, University of Maryland, College Park, USA.

Anne Reese Carswell is WETATi
"IF I CAN HELP SOMEONE, THEN I KNOW MY LIFE WAS WORTH IT."

This book will not be complete in *my book* if I fail to mention in my lifetime another powerful and compassionate woman who has achieved the impossible but also epitomizes who a WETATi woman is. I have met a lot of women who qualify to be WETATians, but then there are those who go the extra mile to distinguish themselves in another class of empowered women – a class made up of women about whom you cannot underestimate their power because of how they acquired it, how long they have stayed with it and how they have dispensed of it like our 'President to be' Madam Hillary Clinton. My interest in writing about Ms. Carswell in this book is not only because it is the right book and forum for her to be a part of, but because her life's work parallels that of Hillary's, and most importantly to show the wide caliber of women achieving the impossible in their respective positons. In other ways, this is a woman that I have had the privilege and honor to know and work with 'up close and personal'. Over the length of the years that I have come to know Ms. Carswell, she has exuded in her own right every single one of the 52 reasons why Hillary is WETATi. Therefore, I don't need to re-hash those points again here; rather, let me give you a glimpse into the very special, unique and exceptional human gift that Ms. Carswell is for those who are fortunate enough to encounter her. I also would like to point out that unlike most women, she is not afraid to embrace and support another strong woman.

Like Hillary Clinton, Ms. Carswell is a WETATian who has achieved the impossible in many facets of her life and work; because she too started and has devoted and dedicated her entire life and career to helping children and students, girls and women, locally, nationally and internationally for over 38 years. She does it quietly and behind the scenes and doesn't care who gets the credit and is equally tireless about it.

Ms. Carswell in character is like wine that tastes better with time; the longer you know her, the "sweeter" she gets. The first time I heard her say what her motto is, I wondered if that is really true or perhaps she might be like many others out there who say things for the moment. When Ms. Carswell says, *"If I can help someone, then I know my life was worth it. "*, I knew I needed to get closer to test her without her knowing it. I can report that not only does she 1000% live by that motto every day, but the spirit with which she does live it daily is unprecedented. If this sounds too good to be true, you have got to meet and know Ms. Carswell, and you will understand. For a very long time I was thinking that I got lucky for her kindness toward me, but then I started meeting hundreds of students at the University of Maryland, College Park and others in the community who would say things about her that blew me away. When Hillary Clinton says that it takes a village to raise a child, Ms. Carswell not only understands that, but takes part in it daily. In fact, I have heard students call her their mother away from home. And that she is…and I can see at times how she could be better in some instances. In appreciation of her unwavering commitment to the wellbeing of the students at the University of Maryland, College Park we named the WETATi scholarship fund in her name. It's called the WETATi-Anne Reese Carswell Scholarship Fund through which we give scholarships to schools annually.

Like Hillary Clinton, Ms. Carswell's lifework is all about helping others, unconditionally and regardless of where they are from or what they look like, what they have or don't have. If you see her, you would not believe her age because she does not look like the woman who has done all of these things and is still going strong. Like Clinton she is not a whiner or complainer. She is a problem solver and takes everyone's problem personally and does something about it without regard to how she can benefit and does not make you feel bad that she is helping you. In fact, you have to beg her to take a cup of water from you. She will say 'no' and tell you to keep it for later. I thought about Ms. Carswell during the Democratic Convention when so many people came out to talk about how Hillary Clinton has helped them behind the scenes over the years. I immediately thought about Ms. Carswell because she is the same way.

Ms. Carswell did not just overcome the odds and become the bedrock for the students at the university; she also personally overcame incredible odds as a young woman from the South, being the last born of 10 children and what they had to go through in those years. She is very smart and full of joy – traits that need to be 'bottled' for the rest of the world. I am hopeful that someday her life's success story and accomplishments will be made into a movie for others to learn from her just what it really takes to be a servant of the people. Another very important attribute of Ms. Carswell as a true WETATian is that she is a movement and not a monument in her position unlike so many others out there. Sometimes, when I am in her office and those streams of students come in, I see her face light up as they are asking for help with one thing or the other and she always finds creative ways to meet their needs. Some even come by because they are hungry and have nothing to eat. She makes sure they have something to eat and she makes them feel special for coming to her.

I am very thankful to God for giving me this divine opportunity to bring the virtues of Hillary Clinton to light and now giving me the opportunity to tell the world in a permanent document about another community and world-reaching warrior and WETATian, Ms. Anne Reese Carswell.

For these reasons and more, Ms. Anne Reese Carswell is a woman who has achieved the impossible, and I hereby crown her a full-fledged WETATian. #WETATi Power!